Still Life With Politics

Also by Reg Darling

Coyote Soul, Raven Heart: Meditations of a Hunter-Wanderer

Hartwell Road

A Story of One's Own

Still Life With Politics

Dispatches from the Old Normal

Reg Darling

For Stan

Contents

Bartleby's Rainbow

The autumn day's brightness seemed as substantial as the Earth itself. The road angled up a steep slope across the slowly healing scar of a tornado blowdown that opened the view to a broad expanse of forested valley and vast sky strewn with feathery wisps of high cirrus clouds. As I approached the top of the ridge, scattered clouds from horizon to horizon lit up in rainbow. At first, the patches of rainbow seemed as random as the distribution of clouds across the sky. But then, I imaginatively connected the pieces, and they formed a continuous arc, a whole rainbow. In that moment of realization, everything—my life, humanity's collective love and madness, the weird dance of chaos and order that is the world's wild mysteriousness—all fit together in a moment of perfect, ineffable coherence. The angle of light shifted with my forward-driven motion, the rainbow vanished, and I drove on.

My attention returned to the road and the voice of Tom Waits on the car stereo, "You got to get behind the mule in the morning and plow."

I Didn't Need a Weatherman

Part One

In the spring of 1968, I briefly emerged from the semi-reclusive life of my freshman year to volunteer in Eugene McCarthy's presidential primary campaign. Distributing campaign literature downtown the day after Martin Luther King's assassination, I offered a flier to a middle-aged man who said, "I don't give a shit about that, but I'd sure like to shake the hand of the man who shot that goddamned nigger." I had already gotten several similar, though less vehement, responses that day. I returned to my room, my books, and my solitude. It would take far more than fliers handed out by polite kids with fresh haircuts to penetrate the indifference and blind, bigoted anger of Appalachia.

[I was a student at Clarion State College—now Clarion University—in northwestern Pennsylvania.]

When the spring semester ended, I needed a summer job. After a week filled with a seemingly endless stream of application forms, I had two offers. One of them was with a company that manufactured parts for bomb detonators on a military contract. The alternative was a potato chip factory.

[With the war in Vietnam in full raging stagger, the choice seemed like a no-brainer.]

At the application interview, I was asked if I could count to one hundred. They had a shortage of workers who could do that, and the foremen had better things to do than counting crates of potatoes and barrels of waste.

[A friend got a summer job at a slaughterhouse where he spent his workdays shooting pigs in the head with a .22. He said he got used to it. It occurred to me that perhaps some things shouldn't be gotten used to, but I didn't tell him that.]

My primary responsibility was the operation of an automatic potato peeler. I stood on a three-foot square metal grate platform. A steel hopper protruded through the wall just above eye level to my left. The peeler, about the size of a fifty-five gallon drum, stood directly in front of me; its abrasive inner surface spun rapidly while a jet of water continually flushed the mix of potato peelings and starch out the bottom into metal grate-covered drainage trenches in the concrete floor. To my right, on the bottom of the peeler, was a hatch that opened onto a conveyer leading to the rest of the production line: slicer, fryer, and packaging machines.

My job was to press a button on the side of the hopper with my left hand; this filled the hopper with potatoes from a much larger hopper in the warehouse area on the other side of the wall. Then, I lifted a latch and swung open a metal door, spilling a load of potatoes into the peeler, closed and latched the door, and pressed the button again. After a few seconds, I bent down, opened the hatch in the bottom of the peeler, released the potatoes onto the conveyor belt, and closed the hatch. Then I opened the hopper to dump more potatoes into the peeler, pressed the button to refill the hopper, let the peeled potatoes out onto the conveyor belt, and so on for nine hours per day with two ten-minute coffee breaks and a half hour for lunch.

On my first day, one of the regular workers came by and asked how I was doing.

"Okay," I said.

"Yeah, it ain't so bad once you get the hang of it," he replied.

[A fair number of my fellow workers seemed stunted and dim, and those who didn't carried an indefinable aura of damage. Whether their dimness was a birthright or an accumulation of scars was neither relevant nor any of my business. Hard labor and bad luck were the common ground they all stood upon. It wasn't possible to be smug in my ability to count to one hundred. These men had tough lives and lived those lives with more courage than life had ever summoned from me, so at lunchtime, instead of retreating to some quiet corner with a book, I joined the whole crew in the lunchroom and mostly listened.]

There were three production lines, and each fryer held forty thousand gallons of cooking oil. The temperature in the frying room, where the peelers were located, was always around a hundred degrees. The heat and monotony were a simple matter of day-by-day endurance, but the potatoes themselves were another story.

They were stored in bulk in a cool, and dark, but not refrigerated, warehouse. The wooden crates dumped by forklift into the large hopper that fed the smaller one I filled by pressing a button were often as not filled with a brown gelatinous mass of reeking decay, seething with maggots. A fine mist of atomized potato rot and pulverized maggots stained my clothing brown by the end of each day. The smell was indescribable.

Occasionally, I worked fast in order to load the conveyor to capacity and give myself enough time to run back to the warehouse and plead with a forklift operator to find a clean crate or two to provide me a brief respite. But since the flow of potatoes from my end affected the whole production line, doing that always risked inciting the wrath of the fryer operator.

[I came home one day in early June, reeking of rot and maggots, to find my mother weeping in front of the television because Bobby Kennedy had been shot.]

At least once per week, standing in the peeler's foul spray, feeling a surge of near panic, I gave myself permission to walk off the job and never go back. But that self-granted permission enabled me to stay. I was not trapped.

I quit a week before the beginning of the fall semester, to wash the reek and filth out of my lungs, hair, and brain with reading, archery, and long walks. I had enough money to cover textbooks, tuition, late-night diner food, dates, and a thirty-five millimeter camera. My parents paid for my room and cafeteria meal ticket.

I had sat through three months of lunches listening to half-broken men talk about lives so stunted and diminished by hardship and absurdity it made me ache. I had watched the whole glorious, exhilarating uprising of hope that began with Eugene McCarthy go down the toilet. To see society as a nice, cozy place to settle into, placidly do whatever jobs fate delivered, raise a family, and grow old was no longer possible. It all seemed too much like standing on my three-foot square steel platform amidst the spray of rot and corruption swirling up from the depths of the machinery. I wanted off the platform and out of the factory and if I could throw a brick in the works on the way out, so much the better.

I had only one chance to hunt that fall—the final day of the season.

[Hunting mattered. For a redneck male, it was the umbilical connection to home.]

The territory was loved and familiar so I knew where to go and found my opportunity by midmorning. I blew the shot and lost the arrow. Feeling discouraged, I hiked back to Aunt Gert and Uncle Ed's for lunch and saw my father emerge from the woods dragging a doe and smiling broadly. He, too, had missed a deer earlier, but disappointment only sharpened his focus rather than diminishing it. I picked up my bow and quiver and returned to the woods with rekindled determination.

After a half hour of motionless vigilance near a well-traveled deer trail, a lone doe angled across the open, grassy forest, walking slowly. At her closest point, which was still a little too far, I swung with her next step and released the bowstring. The shot felt instantly wrong, and the arrow struck her hindquarter. The broadhead shattered the hip joint. The deer went down, rolled over, rose unsteadily to her feet, and fell again. I drew another arrow from the quiver—I had two left now—and shot again as the doe struggled to her feet once more. The shot was well aimed, but the deer fell again before the arrow flew through the space she had formerly occupied and embedded itself in a tree. I had one arrow left and no room for mistakes.

I walked quickly toward the deer. As I drew near, she stopped struggling and looked at me with dark, frightened eyes shining with the same light of pure sentience that had shone from the eyes of beloved animals who had saved me from drowning in the dark childhood loneliness of my parents crazy, desperate dysfunction. My heart knew this, but circumstance required me to refuse such tender recognition. At three feet, just out of hoof range, I drew the bow and drove an arrow through her heart. She gasped and died. I sat a while with shaking hands and heavy breath to apologize to the deer and to the forest before beginning the work of field dressing and dragging.

While I sat by a campfire that night, a raccoon walked into the outer perimeter of the firelight. Something was terribly wrong with his face. I picked up my bow, stood up, and nocked an arrow. He just stood there. The arrow struck under his chin, exited his belly, and skipped into the dark woods. The raccoon took two calm steps and fell over. He had been shot in the face with a rifle. The bullet had struck at an oblique angle, glanced off his skull, and took out an eye. The wound was horribly infected. I borrowed a shovel from Ed to bury him. My father helped with the digging. He was a terrible presence in my dreams for weeks afterward.

[The realization that the very focal point of success itself could be an agonizing hardship rippled out through my life like waves from a pebble tossed into a still pond.]

Part Two

The war in Vietnam and all the strange liberations, contractions, double binds, and paranoia that went with its time reshaped important aspects of my psyche in several successive phases. The initial ones really can't be non-tritely described because that time is laden with notions and images that mutated into semi-caricature as they were absorbed into popular culture-lite—a universally known narrative that isn't so much directly false as polished to a suspicious gloss. I think it suffices to say that in the process of becoming a conscious adult in the confluence of counterculture, civil rights, and the peace movement, I wallowed in the zeitgeist, including the suburbs of its dark side. Though much of my outward persona was far more superficial than it seemed at the time, the tribal identity that can be supported by the ornaments we choose and refuse to wear is not trivial. For many of us it transformed a pathway out of an obsolete identity from a confusing slog through a morass of hormones and ambiguity into a light leap across a muddy ditch.

[It didn't take long to discover that one could still step in dog shit on the other side.]

I loved the warm embrace of hippie subculture and of gentle, pretty women without makeup or bras, who smelled of patchouli and marijuana smoke. I believed in peace, but I also knew that violence wasn't merely political, that it was deeply embedded in all our souls.

[I had already gotten to know violence from several viewpoints, including my own personal darkness.]

Speaking out against the war was the only way to resist the complicity that pervaded my life.

Acid's alternative paradigm that the body is a complex array of sense organs whose purpose is to understand the world around us, to make sense of the world, danced in perfect harmony with rock and roll's simple, raw message that the body is a manifestation of the divine. Beyond the intentions of the musicians, beyond even the listener's ecstasy, there was truth, transcendence, and divinity in the music. There was the awesome, inevitable, by-God-orgasmic reality of raw being throbbing and pulsing with the immensity of now.

[Fuck the rest. Screw the debates, analytical arguments, and academic rigor —explain this guitar riff, explain this orgasm, explain why this young woman's eyes lay waste to Kant and Hegel.]

Despite its core of conscience and nobility, the antiwar movement harbored its fair share of egotism and folly. Dumb fuckitude is a basic part of the human condition. If we had a means of accurately measuring it, dumb fuckitude in any segment of humanity would probably graph out on a Bell Curve like everything else in the world.

[It's important not to allow the constant background level of human dysfunction to obscure the vital principles of truth and compassion that must be our navigational headings if we are to have any hope of transcending our savagery.]

We grabbed the truth right by the ass, but we hadn't expected it to be so easy to catch. We reacted like the hormonal disasters we mostly were and fucked it up. Though this was partly due to an excess of weed and wine, we would have done much better with parents whose spirits had not been trampled and ravaged by war.

[Sometimes I attempted to have real discussions with my father, but he was lost without the swift guidance of adrenaline rage. I sought a simple revealing of his experience, but he always retreated behind a wall of euphemism and opinion. I was grateful for his material generosity, but continually reinventing him was painfully tiresome.]

While we laughed, danced, fucked, and smoked, the Grim Reaper stood quietly in the background dressed in red, white, and blue.

[Reality became something fluid, flowing, and mutable.]

After close encounters with several kinds of official and unofficial human ugliness, I began to think that flower power needed thorns and teeth. People like me—the battered children of war-damaged fathers—could be that. I could be a sharp tooth, a claw. Having grown up hunting, fishing, hiking, and camping, I had skills my mostly city-bred comrades lacked.

But my brief foray into the wild illegal side of resistance en route to revolution taught me that heavy risk and moral ambiguity make shitty roommates. I had a survival instinct not merely for my beating heart and breathing lungs, but for my truest sense of self.

[Years later, stoned and drunk by a late night campfire, I began to tell an old trusted friend about things I had done in a context of protest that I had never spoken about to anyone. Even drunk or tripping with my most trusted friends, I said nothing. At the first glimpse of detail, he realized where I was going and said, "Shut up! Don't tell anyone—not ever. Talking about that stuff is a line you can't ever afford to cross."]

Cynicism festered like an infection in the wound inflicted at Kent State. Hope retreated from the larger world and took up residence in the realm of living hidden. I continued to provide deserters and draft resisters traveling the underground or en route to Canada a place to crash and a meal, but I didn't want to be a leader or spokesperson. I no longer wanted to be visible. I sensed bad weirdness afoot.

[Fear killed the anarchy in many hearts. Beer and money replaced anger with apathy. But not for everyone—for those who had forest, desert, mountains, or ocean in their hearts, the anarchy went too deep. We hid, waiting for the wild to rise again.]

I recognized the envelope and knew what it meant before I opened it. I was summoned to report for a pre-induction draft physical. I didn't know why my student deferment had been denied and feared that an appeal would only attract unwanted attention. It could easily have been an innocuous bureaucratic glitch, but my fears weren't irrational.

[As loves unraveled in the weird dance of my irremediably vulnerable heart and a young redneck male's hormonal ruthlessness cast suddenly adrift in the strange, wonderful liberations of the times, I had often been uncertain that I did, indeed, want to live. I drifted along not actually seeking death (or not very hard, anyway), but doubting how much I would do to get out of the way if I saw it coming.

But to have my life seized, held, and ruthlessly used seemed vastly worse than merely losing my life to a careless automobile or the happenstance of disease. A compound fractured arm in high school had awakened me to life's inescapable precariousness. There was a lot of random ugly shit floating around in the world and most, but not all, of it could be avoided with a quick wit and good reaction time.]

Though explosive, red-faced shouting matches between my father and I were common, behind our conflicts there was never any doubt that he would lay down his life for me in a heartbeat.

"Where do you want to go? Canada, Sweden—you name it and we'll get you there. I didn't get shot five times in World War II so they could do this to my sons."

"I'm looking at my alternatives. I might not have to leave."

"Just let me know what you need. They'll have to shoot me to take you."

He meant it.

I consulted like-minded people about safe places to crash for three different routes to Canada, but Aaron had a different idea. "Check the queer box," he said.

"What do you mean?"

"There's a checklist of various physical and mental conditions on the form you'll have to fill out at the physical. One of them is 'homosexual tendencies'—put a checkmark there."

"Won't they question me?"

"Of course they will. Keep your answers simple. Answer with just yes or no as much as possible. Don't tell a story. If you have to name a witness or lover, use my name."

Though Aaron was utterly confident his plan would work, I considered other alternatives. Applying for conscientious objector's status was too risky. Any plan that involved calling attention to myself could undermine other options, leaving me trapped if it failed. I could buy a black market kidney stone. They came with a list of symptoms and instructions on what to tell one's doctor. It was only a temporary reprieve. It was rumored that eating several tablespoons of Tide before the physical would dramatically elevate your blood pressure. If you didn't have a stroke, you would have a few months to figure out what to do next—another temporary reprieve.

[I didn't want a temporary reprieve. I wanted this shit off my back and out of my life.]

I could go to Canada. The problem, of course, was that I might well never be able to return. Exile had to be a last resort.

[My heart was rooted in the forests of home.]

Several of my fellow anti-war activists thought I should refuse the draft as an act of civil disobedience and willingly go to prison to protest the savage injustice of the war. I believed my first and foremost duty with regard to the war was to refuse to participate, but could see no great nobility or political effectiveness in being punished for my refusal. In fact, I thought the best political statement I could make would be to refuse and not be punished. I was also pissed off and personally unwilling to voluntarily surrender any part of my life to the evil swine who had led my country into senseless war. With regard to my life, their impotence would be my protest.

[If I walked away from my refusal unscathed, every orgasm, toke, and hike would be a joyous celebration of disobedience.]

For me, the war and the draft were separate issues. Military conscription is nothing more than a specialized form of slavery—I would have dodged the draft in peacetime. I believed that if someone tried to abduct me for the purpose of placing me in involuntary servitude, I would be morally justified in resisting by any means at my disposal, including lethal force, if necessary. I was not a pacifist and I would not submit. Going to prison for refusing to be a slave would be an act of submission, not resistance. I had my life, and I intended to live it. Dodging the draft was not a protest—it was self-defense.

[Freedom is not a copout; it's a birthright.]

I made contacts and studied routes. If Aaron's plan didn't work, Canada was Plan B. I would cross over via Vermont, Minnesota, or Washington.

I spent the day before the physical at Aaron's cabin getting briefed. He mapped out the basic ground rules: Keep to yourself. Don't get drawn into conversations. Keep it simple. Answer with yes or no whenever possible. Don't tell a story, because that only creates a risk of getting caught in a contradiction. Smile and be polite. At random moments during conversation about other things, Aaron would fire a potential draft physical question at me and critique my answer. I was provisionally confident.

If I had any misgivings about evading the draft, the pre-induction physical erased them quickly. It was terrifyingly obvious that the prospective inductees were on a production line. We were abstract units, pieces of meat. I would never allow this military machine to control my life. If Aaron's gambit failed, I would do whatever I had to do to resist. If I had to go underground or head for the border, I would be armed until the very last feasible point to ditch the weapons before crossing.

[Would I have resorted to violence had I encountered official, or even unofficial, interference? Well, in 1970 I was a very righteously pissed-off young man, so yes, there's a fair chance things could have gotten ugly. Now, many years later, I realize that the person whose work it would be to stop me is probably just someone with a job and friends and family—trying to navigate through this world mostly by dumbass guesswork, just like me, someone I could probably enjoy having a beer with. The situation would be neck deep in moral ambiguity. So, I would like to say that violence is something I've cast aside.

The problem is that my son was a college student when Dubya cooked up his scam war in Iraq. When it started, I consulted like-minded people about travel routes and safe places to stay for three different ways out of the country. The draft was never reinstated, but if it had been, my son would have had an armed escort to the border. Though that isn't macho bluster, I find it a bit embarrassing to talk about because it sounds uncomfortably similar to the ranting of people I think of as utter whack-jobs. But I was not delusional to think that the government might declare it expedient to seize my kid for cannon fodder, and in that circumstance, submission would be unthinkable.]

The realization that the government could snatch my life away, and when I got too old to be optimally useful, it could snatch my children or grandchildren and send them off to kill and die in the third-world shithole of its choice, imprinted me in a fairly indelible way.

An idealistic friend said, "This isn't about you."

"The hell it isn't," I replied.

Beyond all the intricate lunacies of national and international politics, it was clear that the government was attempting to seize my life. It was time to take this personally.

So I was very focused. After all the assorted standard physical checks, we were herded into a large holding area where we waited to be called for individual attention relating to items checked on our forms, selected by the Marines, or sent home. I sat quietly apart from the others, simmering with rage and determination.

The interview with the "shrink" (I have no idea what his real qualifications were) was fairly easy. He seemed more nervous than I. His whole demeanor bespoke a thinly disguised mixture of disgust and fear.

"I can't tell by looking at you or talking to you if this is true. How do I know this is true?"

"If it wasn't true, I wouldn't have signed it. It says right here you can go to jail for lying."

"When was your last homosexual experience?"

"Last night."

"Are you depressed about this?"

"Sometimes."

"Have you ever dated women?"

"Yes."

"How do you explain that?"

"I have lots of tendencies."

"Have you ever used illegal drugs?"

"Yes."

"Would you be willing to sign a statement?"

"Yes, but isn't that what I just did?"

He sent me back to the waiting area, and an hour later they let everyone go.

A few weeks afterward, I was notified that my draft status had been changed to 1-Y. I was free.

[I was also desperate.]

The realization that there were sinister forces at large in the world that could take people like me into custody and either lock us in cages or enslave us in duty to the military (which could involve the wholesale slaughter of innocent people for ill-defined political reasons) was an exponentially altered view of the world and my possible future in it.

Though I had been a battered child, I had also been strangely sheltered by my parents' dysfunction. I thought one could take for granted one's right to simply follow the convoluted flow of life, love, desire, and spirit.

[Truth is an invention, which is why the inventing of it is so hugely important.]

Now, knowing that beneath and behind the grit of wage labor and the lovely shivers of art and sex lurked a cold mechanized threat aroused a complex mixture of reactions with anger and dread being high on the list. I had to be ornery, vigilant, skeptical, and prepared if I wanted to retain possession of my own life.

My country had declared war on me. We achieved a ceasefire of sorts, but our peace has remained unstable and uncertain.

[Lately, it has taken a turn for the worse.]

I had to evolve a new, strange, complex morality in order to walk out the other side of this slow-motion kidnap attempt alive and free. I was already capable of an innocent ruthlessness that I hadn't yet recognized as appalling, but my personal collision with the draft system was truly a loss of innocence.

[I realized I was higher on the food chain in the forest than in town.]

There was a tough vigilance that I would have to hold to for the rest of my life. I would always be ready to disappear, and for a while, that possibility was relatively easy to maintain. My Pleistocene vigilance faded apace with obvious necessity despite the lingering background knowledge that the spirit of Tricky Dick on meth still roams America, howling.

The loss of innocence was far deeper than the terrible blunders of love and sex. The draft notice changed me and, mostly not for the better, even though those changes may also have saved me more than once.

I would always be an outlaw, even at my law-abiding best, and there was no remedy for it. There were fundamental ways of regarding one's relationship with one's country and government that were no longer possible for me. I became an outsider in ways that could never be fully remedied.

I was also extraordinarily angry and though my rage was largely justified, I already had a sufficient supply of dark anarchy in my heart. Adding more neither improved nor protected my life—all it did was juice up the PTSD and reclassify a big chunk of my heart's darkness as a primarily political problem.

I was willing to have a ceasefire with my government because I had other work to do that was more important than anything even remotely likely to result from entangling my life in some sort of revolutionary martyrdom. But I would never sign a treaty.

[Those motherfuckers had crossed the line in a big way.]

It's not like you can try to abduct and enslave someone for the purpose of using them as a disposable weapon and when you fail to bring it off you can just say, "Oops, sorry about that," and everything is peachy again.

I assembled "The Box" and kept it close.

The contents of the box:

A file folder containing a new identity, including a valid social security number, a loaded handgun, twenty-five rounds of ammunition, waterproof matches, a compass, a hunting knife, a small flashlight, with extra batteries, twenty feet of nylon cord, and $500.00 in cash.

I never showed the box to anyone. Its necessity gave permission to the harboring of secrets. The possibility of needing the box rendered all commitments provisional to some indefinable degree that I preferred not to think about and still cannot assess.

I don't want to overdramatize—it's not like I was afraid all the time. I was really pretty confident in the way wild young males tend to be, and my fondness for marijuana had cultivated a matter-of-fact tolerance for paranoia. All hippies lived with a certain level of day-to-day fear (we often carried felonies in our pockets), and I just had a little more that couldn't be flushed or swallowed. After a while, it became almost normal. I kept my fear in the box, and I kept the box because the fear leaked out whenever I thought about ditching it.

The box followed me for more than a decade. The handgun got unloaded when I became a parent. I told my wife about the basics, but skipped the details. Though I had intended to shred or burn it, my spare identity got stashed away with old journals and forgotten long before the Internet age rendered it hopelessly obsolete. And then, in the waning days of 2016, with Amerika gone weird and stupidly narrow, it resurfaced with eerie timeliness when I was looking for something else, as such things tend to do.

I tossed the yellowed file folder into the fireplace and watched it burn.

[That my dissidence could have been wilder and stronger is a guilt I still carry.]

Pennsyltucky Expat

The Alleghenies are sometimes called mountains by outsiders (flatlanders), hills by insiders. Both descriptions miss the way it feels to be there. It is a place of valleys. Geologically, it is an eroded plateau. The slopes weren't formed by slow crumpling or urgent quakes. The ridges exist not by fault, but by default. The land was shaped by the persistent polish of rain. The violence of tectonics is conspicuously absent.

[A quiet mind can feel this.]

Allegheny wildness is defined by the enfolding gentleness of forested valley spaces. The recumbent masses of ridge and confluence caress the eye with wind-sighed resemblances that invite embrace and disdain conquest. The voices of wind and light are soothingly soft, but quartz conglomerate outcrops first laid down by glacial water, then hidden by forest decay and revealed anew by rain whisper an ancient urgency of ice and flood. Strata of smooth, round quartz pebbles encircle the hills like impossibly abundant pearls. There is an extraordinarily gentle magnificence in this soft-spoken land of hard-spoken people.

[A boondock suburb of Appalachia, currents of weird anger flow in the blood of its culture.]

In the late nineteenth and early twentieth centuries, the hills and valleys of northwestern Pennsylvania were ravaged for oil and lumber. Both the pious and the wild were laborers in the paroxysm of mindless industrial greed that shaped America into gluttonous empire. In places defined by space and wildness, they saw only absence into which they could pour their greed, which was widely regarded as a civic virtue.

[They treated their women poorly and knew not what they did.]

The nineteenth-century notion that nature's bounty was endless and existed only for human use was a universal, unspoken cultural subtext.

[This still lingers in the twenty-first century.]

Though many felt the comforting peace of the forest, cherished its healing powers, and loved its glimpses of holiness, nothing connected those feelings to a larger sense of how to live individually and collectively, to earning a living, to politics. They lacked the contemplative luxury to recognize the possibility of becoming truly native to their land. They were just trying to get by.

[The people's shared sense of peasantry pervaded even the gentry.]

The Great Depression knocked local culture back into the frontier mentality it had only begun to climb out of by the 1920s.

[And then the world went to war.]

I was born in the Alleghenies just in time to define myself by wandering through the peak of the land's recovery. In the forest, I found the renewing energy I needed to heal the inner wounds inflicted by a war-damaged father and a batshit crazy mother. The forest absorbed my sorrow because its own wounds directed its ambient energies into healing. This is how I survived.

[The economy's brutal relationship with its circumambient beauty was paralleled by its disrespect for the possible epiphanies of its peoples' hearts.]

But the people mostly remained rooted in subservience to extractive industry. Heedless exploitation is the paradigm embedded at the core of their stunted culture. The collective worldview is zero sum—human prosperity only comes from a righteous diminishment of nature.

[The second half of my trajectory wasn't as well timed as the first.]

Now, the hills are being gnawed to mud and crude roads. The land is awash with the buzzing of chainsaws and ATVs. Hydrofracturing is rampant. The forest is brain shot and twitching. Gas and oil stand poised to gut it and drag it home. The patriotic locals are eagerly hoping to gnaw on the bones. They love Jesus, fast cars, and the word 'freedom' when it is hammer-forged with humorless irony into a chain.

[I live in Vermont now. It's not Shangri-La, but the battered wildness of my heart feels safer here.]

Setting the Hook

I was getting as many bites as the others, but kept missing when I tried to set the hook. My father, who was typically more inclined to bask in the obvious superiority of his own technique than to seize a teachable moment, found my frustration mildly amusing. Uncle Ed, on the other hand, wasn't interested in comparison or competition. He said, "Just do as I say—let me know when you feel a bite."

A few minutes passed.

"Okay…something's taking it now."

"Let him have it…"

The rod tip bent distinctly.

"Just let him take it," Ed reiterated.

"Hold on a little longer…now jerk it hard—break his goddamned neck!"

I did as I was told and hauled in a nice-sized perch, bent and quivering because I probably had, indeed, broken "his goddamned neck."

On through that and subsequent days, I refined my technique with ample natural incentive: extracting swallowed hooks is messy, difficult, and cruel. I worked back from too much to enough, rather than groping blindly forward from inadequacy underlined by my father's visibly relished competitive success. When I arrived at enough, I found it subtle, elegant, and strangely gentle in ways that mirrored Ed's gentlemanly urbane manner strangely juxtaposed with his wild, anarchic heart and his daily bottle of whiskey. He was a wiser man than even he realized.

Still Life With Politics

I wrapped up the interviews on my list of rural route addresses quicker than expected. But the last one shattered my composure.

It took place in a house of such raw, stark filth that merely witnessing it bruised the spirit. An old woman in the household had cut her leg with an ax. The four-inch gash was red, swollen, and festering. Her son, an arrogant, unwashed lout who stank of gasoline and stale sweat, was proud of the new outhouse he had built thirty yards uphill from the spring that supplied their drinking water. I wanted to tell him the crazed, babbling old woman should be taken to the hospital, but I knew better. The heat and stench were suffocating. There was a dead cat in the nearly full kitchen garbage can—it was not fresh.

After I got their signatures on the appropriate forms, I fled to a friend's country home. He was working in his garden, and I picked up a hoe and joined him.

Doing real, tangible work was like gulping fresh air after nearly suffocating.

We took a break for cold beer and raw kohlrabi he peeled and sliced with his pocketknife. I stayed for dinner, and afterward, we built a campfire.

I awoke the next morning with crusted oozing sores on my face.

The doctor said, "You have staph infection."

"How would I have gotten that?' I asked.

"What do you do for a living?"

"I'm a caseworker for the Department of Public Welfare."

"Well then, I guess we know how you got staph infection."

Though I can't claim the kind of penetrating wisdom that would enable an astute analysis of how America came to its present state of frenetic malaise, the presumption that collective responsibility and personal liberty are irreconcilably in conflict—an either/or choice—is rather more than obvious in the shrilly-proclaimed background. You can't choose one without forsaking the other—a simple-minded variation on the classic Christian duality. It is batshit crazy.

I took refuge in the Pleistocene to keep my heart from suffocating in the malaise of state government bureaucracy and the wrecked lives that were my livelihood.

Sitting in fading light on the tundra of northern Quebec beside a friend's freshly killed caribou to keep the wolves away was not a symbolic act, not a ritual.

[I had a bow and homemade wooden arrows—I did not have a gun.]

It had meaning beyond its literal immediacy, meaning that could be interpreted in terms of ritual, ceremony, and the re-experiencing of ancient realities, but the wolves were real and so was the bloody, fragrant meat that nourished our bodies. In the reality of nourishment, blood and symbol converged in the present and echoed into the future.

In the nineteenth and twentieth centuries, the Pleistocene world that shaped our evolution receded into abstraction too rapidly for sensible adaptation.

In places defined by space and wildness, powerful men saw only absence into which they could pour their greed, which was widely regarded as a civic virtue.

[They treated their women poorly and knew not what they did.]

Perhaps we are killing off the wildness in our land with such carelessness, callousness, and greed because it's already dead in our hearts.

Despite their visible woe, the folks who were merely having a rough ride on a stretch of bad luck road were a relief. They would likely be saved by time, probability, and their own resourcefulness, regardless of what I did. Welfare programs kept some of the wounds from leaving deep scars. I could take some bumps out of their road by being courteous and competent. They rarely gave us much to talk or even think about, so even though they were the majority of our clients and were the most fundamental raison d'etre for our jobs, they were invisible in our stories and anonymous in our memories.

[Please remember this often, as you read onward.]

The welfare system worked surprisingly well within the limitations imposed by the political realm.

[I am not a journalist.]

I watched people's souls get fat from lack of exercise—from cheap beer, loveless fucks, unloved work, and a wordless mixture of cowardice and shame. Their sparks of brilliance were pissed upon and pissed away, until what was left was little more than a parody of what their hearts still sincerely pretended to be.

If a client took too much time on the phone, others would call and get put on hold, and the phone would ring again the instant it was put down. On a busy day, one long-winded client could trigger a two- or three-hour chain of continuous phone calls that would leave the caseworker sitting glassy-eyed before a desk littered with case files and scribbled notes. When it happened in fortuitous conjunction with illness, car trouble, romantic complications, or a hangover, the result could be a gut-churning spasm of suppressed panic.

Civilization is a collective enterprise. I don't think I need to lay down tens or hundreds of pages of scholarly erudition and analysis to justify that statement. Every member of the enterprise should get a cut of the profit. Okay? We're talking basic toddler level fairness here.

Daniel, a caseworker who had transferred from an urban county, complained to me that his latest performance evaluation was the worst he had ever received. He was troubled by it, even though it wasn't a bad evaluation, per se. His naive earnestness annoyed me.

[Daniel had transferred to a county of farms and forests in pursuit of a vaguely pastoral way of life that didn't exist.]

I said, "If you think a performance evaluation means diddly shit about you as a person, then your biggest problem is that you need to grow up."

He went home at the end of the day, put the barrel of his .357 magnum in his mouth, and pulled the trigger.

Daniel had far bigger problems than his performance evaluation or my insensitivity, but forgiving myself was difficult and redemption was complicated.

Though in dark moments, the human race seems rather like a swollen-livered drunk on a bender, risking the horrific final shutdown of a too often poisoned body for the sake of the grim, grinding satisfaction of self-pity and forgetfulness, the alternative grim, grinding pleasures of righteous, dystopian fantasy aren't worth a bottle of cheap vodka, and the rapture is bullshit.

[Tomorrow's doom can't negate today's possibilities of kindness.]

We all know it's bullshit, but we're addicted to the sweet, righteous loin stir of wild doom that we, in our luscious personal wisdom, are uniquely able to perceive, predict, avert, embrace, and/or profit from.

Having wrestled with chronic depression all my life, I am well acquainted with the strange seductiveness of doom. I resist it with art and insight, but it could still get me someday.

I refuse the mind-numbing nobility of a Viking Valhalla or any other less testosterone based version of divinity or duty.

The elderly woman repeatedly interrupted the medical assistance interview to scurry into her bathroom and flush the toilet. After several repetitions, she noticed my puzzled expression and explained that she had a six-pack of beer in the toilet tank and needed to keep it cold.

A human being fully living a whole life hunts, gathers wild plants, tends a garden, engages in a practical craft, makes art, feasts with friends, engages in ceremonial practices to cultivate reverence and compassion, tells and listens to stories, makes love, mourns, meditates, and dreams. This is our evolved nature. It is both our right and our responsibility.

My last field interview of the day was a talkative (probably lonely) old couple. The necessary fifteen minutes of medical assistance and food stamp eligibility business rambled past forty-five. I was pleasant, congenial, and supportive—reflective listening, gentle eye contact, etcetera. They were decent people rendered pathetic by old age, diabetes, and bad luck. She looked like she had been pretty once, but now she was fat and smoked unfiltered Camels, while gasping for breath. His back was stooped and his memory faltered. They liked me, and I played the nice young man role to the hilt, while skillfully edging the conversation toward a graceful exit. The weird, sad guilt I once felt in such situations had been replaced by pathos observed from a semi-cool distance. Finished for the day, I retreated to the semidarkness of the Plaza Restaurant to drink strong coffee and write in my journal.

Alienation is an emotional state. If you let it metamorphose into a philosophical principle you're really fucked.

Ira came in every few weeks to angrily accuse me of spying on him. He believed I worked for the CIA, which he was certain had taken an inordinate interest in the details of his daily life, due to unspecified secret things only he knew. But his rants were mercifully brief, and he picked up on my subtle enough to be deniable hints that my secret colleagues in the agency would hunt him down like a dog if he ever harmed me.

Government programs begin in mission-driven idealism, but decay like radioactive isotopes, steadily becoming rule-driven, like uranium turning to lead. The idealism doesn't come from politicians, but from the people who transform legislation into reality—the bureaucrats. It's weird work and bureaucrats burn out—they have a half-life. Completing reports on time becomes the measure of success.

The new caseworker trainee was getting ready to go out on his first home visit. When he told me where he was going, I was shocked that the training supervisor would send a rookie there. He had been assigned to visit a multi-generation welfare family that had sunken to depths far beyond the mundane dysfunctions that justified our jobs. I advised him to conduct the interview in the kitchen, where there were wooden chairs. "Trust me; you don't want to sit on anything stuffed in that house," I said.

He was nervous as he sat at the kitchen table and, as he opened his briefcase, he fumbled and dropped his pen. When he bent down to pick it up, it was sticking in a pile of dog shit. Fortunately, he had brought a spare.

The trainee returned to the office babbling and whining in a mixture of anger, disgust, and near panic. He needed this job—partly enabled by his veteran's preference in civil service hiring, it was a "good job" and his reward for serving in Vietnam. Medical insurance, paid vacation, sick leave, and a retirement program were far more important than disease, despair, and dog shit.

Our animals bless us with opportunities for kindness and in their grace, they teach us the generosity of receiving.

During the office interview with his mother, the dirty, but cheerful four-year-old said, "My mommy made cookies last night."

"That's nice, were they yummy?"

"Yeah, and the rats only got half of them."

While his mother and I completed the interview, he pissed in my garbage can.

The exercise of institutional power, even on a comparatively small scale, tends to corrupt those who wield it. Those who successfully resist corruption tend to be gradually diminished as human beings. Their consciousness lacks fluidity. This is sad, but the sadness isn't the worst part.

The phone rang, and the client immediately began spilling his tale of woe and injustice. He had a good start before I realized he wasn't in my caseload.

"I'm sorry, but I'm not your caseworker. I think it would be best if you spoke to him directly. Hold on and I'll transfer your call."

I transferred the call to the caseworker I thought should have the case and who sat at the desk next to mine. After a moment, I heard him say, "I'm sorry, I'm not your caseworker; please hold while I transfer your call." The call was picked up by a caseworker across the room who, after a moment said, "I'm sorry, I don't have your case; please hold on."

At that point, another caseworker said aloud, with audible disgust in his voice, "Just transfer the call to me, and I'll deal with it. At least there's one adult in this room."

He picked up his phone, but by this time the client was seriously frustrated. The caseworker's eyes widened, and his body stiffened as the client ranted. "Fuck you, too," he said and slammed the phone down.

Let's face it, there's no real, functional or moral difference between being a worker for Exxon, or General Electric, or Archer, Daniels, Midland and being a peasant under the rule of the Archduke of Analprobia in 1150 AD. Sure, folks nowadays are mostly better off in all the obvious ways (as are the Archdukes), but their share of the fruits of the collective labor that consumes their lives compared to the nobility's share is no better. It's a raw deal, but we are collectively too docile and obedient to discuss it.

[We're willing to talk and even argue passionately about almost anything but the emperor's hairy naked ass.]

Those wielding the power of money are so shameless in their smug confidence in the folly and ignorance of the masses that they'll look us straight in the eye and tell us their obscenely disproportionate profits make the whole enterprise of civilization noble.

The woman insisted her husband had no handicaps or disabilities. His baseball cap was festooned with a dozen or more pins, all bearing images of skulls. He had difficulty continuing a single conversational direction beyond a sentence or two. At age thirty-two, he had never held a job for more than a few days. He bathed every two or three months, whether he needed it or not.

I explained that it would be beneficial to the whole family if he could qualify for a disability-related category of assistance.

"Has he ever had any kind of problem that might affect his ability to work," I asked.

"Well, he hears voices."

"Has he seen a doctor about that?"

"Yeah, the doctor told him not to listen to them."

A few weeks later, one of the voices identified itself as God and told him his wife was in league with Satan in a plot to destroy him. He chased her down the street with a butcher knife.

She forgave him for the sake of their children, and he qualified for disability.

The social/political/economic car is going really fast and we the people are not in the driver's seat. Helping each other cope with this situation requires exponentially more than the deep neighborliness of an isolated village. It requires a government to function as an agent of our collective responsibilities.

[Non-military collective responsibilities are politically unpopular these days. In a zero-sum world, individual rights gain a lot of traction over collective responsibilities.]

The previous caseworker had told me, when she transferred the case, that the client had hinted at suicide in her previous two interviews. I scheduled a home visit for her eligibility review (food stamps and Medicaid) to spare her the presumed stress of an office interview.

The not quite elderly woman had a distinct eastern European accent and spoke openly of her overwhelming weariness with life. I did my clumsy, awkward, aging hippie best to be compassionate while steering the conversation back to the business at hand—income, assets, rent, utilities, medical bills, etcetera. When all the documents had been reviewed and papers signed, I delivered my standard recitation about when she would receive a letter notifying her of any changes, her right to appeal, and my unofficial assessment that there likely would be no adverse changes in her benefits. She said it was time to end her life anyway. I said something upbeat and horridly trite and left.

During the short drive back to the office, I began to process what I had to do. I completed the appropriate paperwork and called the sheriff's office to initiate a court-ordered commitment. It was the procedurally and (it seemed) ethically proper thing to do. A person who will tell their caseworker in their first interview that they're going to off themselves needs professional help. Right?

All I had known about her background was what I could infer from her accent and social security income from a deceased husband. Later, I learned that the root of her depression was her childhood experience of having the Gestapo drag her and her family out of their home and ship them to a concentration camp, where the rest of the family perished.

When the sheriff's department sent two armed, uniformed officers to take her from her home to the hospital's psychiatric ward, she was beyond terrified.

Blaming a politician for using an important issue to further their own agenda is like blaming a shark for biting a seal. Seriously, it's a fucking tropism. One of the basic problems facing civilization right now is "How do we transcend those of our socially activated tropisms that tend to produce violence, bigotry, fraud, cruelty, and television commercials?" We have to figure out a way to rein that shit in, without sacrificing our freedom. If we continue to succumb to reactionary twitches of self-righteousness and simplistic sloganeering, our grandchildren will drown in bullshit.

This is the other national debt and it's more toxic than borrowed money.

An older, very conservative fellow caseworker lectured me about her disapproval of a case I had opened. "You know, it creates a scandal in town when birds like that are allowed to get welfare."

"My decisions aren't based on a referendum. I opened that case in accord with department policy. If you have a problem with the quality of my work, perhaps you should speak to my supervisor," I replied.

Homo sapiens is a highly erotic species, and being very clever, has managed to win a relatively long lifespan. Since we have good memories and good tools to expand and extend memory, we're able to use that long lifespan to extend itself even farther and further into time. Our evolved bodies are drawn to multiple possibilities of coupling.

[For our species to continue, only a small percentage of our couplings need to result in conception.]

The self-renewing epiphany of love cultivated in an intensely sexual long-term relationship sets a gold standard of sorts for our current, collective definition of "love." There was a time when the defining standard was the love of God. The present situation is an improvement. It is no less vulnerable to sleazy manipulation by power hungry and/or greed-addled miscreants, but the manipulations tend to be less violent and a little more transparent.

That a significant portion of this monogamy is serial, because at least forty percent of us are fucking idiots and, anyway, shit happens, does not negate the social value of monogamy. When monogamy works, it produces a special wisdom that a viable culture needs.

[The multi-layered richness of nuance and meaning that accrues through many years of nurtured commitment and cycles of renewal.]

But culture also needs the wisdom that comes from the various configurations of conflict and compassion produced when monogamy fails.

[The inventiveness and resiliency spawned by the necessity of reinventing oneself.]

In the real world of wild creatures this is called an ecosystem.

Our loving urges are ancient and they are many—this is not difficult to understand.

While I interviewed the matriarch of a multigenerational welfare clan, a teenaged brother and sister were having sex in an adjoining room, with the door open. "I keep telling them not to do that, but they just won't listen," she said.

While intelligent cynicism is easy, being an artist is a bitch. The pervasive subordination of all values, including all the difficult richness of art's possibilities, to an extraordinarily crude economic paradigm tends to level expression to a very low common denominator, indeed.

Corporate industry's environmental rapaciousness renders the heart's natural tendency to love the wondrous particularities of places, both spectacular and obscure, untenably risky for anyone without badly calloused sensitivity, thus divorcing spirituality from its living metaphors in land and personal origin. The resulting dumbed-down dance of crassness and shrunken aspirations has become the norm. Those who need more than the generic soothing of the pathetically provincial are regarded as pretentious and false—unworthy even of the focused attention that ought to be prerequisite to such dismissal. Like the beleaguered trees, artists must take their nourishment from the thinning soil of dying forests.

They sustain themselves with books, drink, and travel.

On my last home visit as a caseworker before my promotion to supervisor, I asked the client, a grizzled old derelict, if he had any expenses for medication.

He reached under the threadbare couch, pulled out a half-empty bottle of cheap whiskey, and held it up with a flourish and a grin.

"Sorry, I can't count that," I said.

He laughed and said, "I didn't think so."

Though there are small-scale entrepreneurs scattered throughout American society, a very large majority of the populace is employed in collective enterprises. This has nothing to do with socialism—it is corporate capitalism. Those who wield the power of money are not inclined to admit that large scale corporate capitalism is simply the control of collective workforces by nongovernmental authority. That the corporate sector is a de facto branch of government isn't discussed.

Corporate profits are created by deducting them from the worker's share of the value added to raw materials by their labor, which doesn't sound much different than a tax. It also looks more and more like feudalism as it becomes steadily more entrenched.

In meetings deeply tainted with foolish internal politics, I learned to argue passionately for things I didn't care about. I also learned to be lied to without being insulted by it. Those two skills were considered to be key elements of professionalism. It was shameful, and I was ashamed of my patience.

Amurka is awash in rants and slogans about rapture, Jayzus, jack-booted thugs, secret Muslim politicians, fascism, socialism, feudalism, corporate aristocracy, etcetera, etcetera, etcetera, ad puke.

Goodness has become an abstraction, but we are not doing battle with Satan's minions. We are trying to eat well and stay warm under a roof that doesn't leak and have a little time left over for play and art. It's a tough job, but we all have to do it.

Why is doing it well not enough?

The true effectiveness of an agency like the Pennsylvania Department of Public Welfare can only be measured on a much longer term than fiscal years or election cycles. Frankly, other than the victims of short-term bad luck and the elderly, there's not much that can be done for the dysfunctional adults that wash ashore in the welfare office lobby. Their dysfunction is deeply ingrained by their late teens and all but hopeless by thirty. They tend to reproduce carelessly. But if you lighten the load for them, you may give their children enough slack to become at least marginally competent parents, thus giving the grandchildren a fair shot at being okay.

To accomplish this on a meaningful scale, it is often necessary to give help and comfort to dirty, dishonest, obnoxious, disgusting, stupid, drunken, and/or crazy people. This is part of the price of mending a tear in the socio-economic fabric. It drives Republicans crazy—understandably so. It stinks. It's not fair. It sucks. Doing that necessary work is miserably stressful no matter how well you understand its dirty necessity, but the alternatives are exponentially worse.

That's how I felt about changing a tire the last time I got a flat, but I still had to change the fucking tire, if I wanted to drive on. The fair isn't until August —this is reality. Gravity sucks when you lose your handhold on a cliff too, but there's nothing and no one to argue with about it.

Caring for the sick, wounded, elderly, and the young and feeding the hungry are fundamental, collective responsibilities of a civilized society. Failure to address those responsibilities is worse than mere neglect, oversight, or incompetence; it is savagery.

In winter woods not far from home, I paused to watch and listen. Two large flocks of trumpeter swans flew over. Silvery white against the pale luminous gray sky of falling snow, they were so exquisitely beautiful that recalling them later sent a shiver down my spine. Their voices sang to my heart with a poignancy that touched all my yearning, all my wandering. Afterward, the sound of falling snow and the creek a hundred yards away defined the surrounding silence. A wave of indescribable sadness and longing swept over me, then passed. Suddenly the sound of rustling leaves, a twig breaking—a whitetail doe came running by, seventy yards out, followed by an ardently grunting buck. They crossed directly downwind, but didn't seem to notice my scent. Freshly alert for a while, I slowly drifted back into the hypnotic reverie of falling snow.

Spring, 1970

Military recruiters set up tables in a hallway in the Administration Building, which also housed the college library. Antiwar activists set up an information table a short distance down the hall in front of the library entrance. Within a few minutes, a college dean (whose name and full title I've forgotten) arrived on the scene and ordered us out of the building, because our presence made the recruiters "uncomfortable."

I said, "I pay tuition—I have more right to be here than they do."

"Are you refusing to leave?"

"Yes."

"Then I'll have to call the police."

"That's a good idea. In fact, I think you should have me arrested."

"…"

I turned to the young woman who was with me, handed her a quarter, and said, "There's a pay phone in the library—call Dr. Van Bruggen."

[Dr. Van Bruggen was a tenured political science professor and chair of the local chapter of the American Civil Liberties Union.]

The dean sighed and said, "All right, you can stay. Don't cause any trouble."

Later, on my way to the Student Union for takeout coffee, I stopped at the recruiters' table to ask if they wanted anything. They said, "No, thanks," but seemed genuinely pleasant and friendly.

[They may also have been afraid I would spike their coffee with drugs.]

The End of the Beginning

When the woman with whom I shared a stormy relationship told me she was pregnant, I said, "However you want to deal with this, I'll help you." It would be easy (and convenient) to simply ascribe my response to love, but there were layers of unspoken complication. She was also having an affair with someone else. I knew about it, but she didn't know that I knew. I hadn't confronted the situation because my own actions gave me little right to self-righteousness. I also feared that forcing our infidelities out into the open would generate more heat than light.

[When dishonesty masquerades as kindness, there is usually cowardice lurking in the shadows.]

I hoped that the innocence of my response would summon greater honesty from her.

[I still trusted her heart.]

She told me that she had already scheduled an abortion at an urban clinic three hours away. I offered to take her there and pay for half. The procedure went smoothly, and we even made a brief stop at an art museum afterward. On the long, silent drive home, I wept silently, unseen tears streaming down my face in the dark.

[I didn't weep for the fetus.]

I wept for an almost childlike sense of abject defeat, for the realization that our relationship had become so fucked up that it probably couldn't be fixed.

Truth was receding from our love like the galaxies of an expanding universe. We could never get it back, but neither could we stop trying until we were rescued by a new betrayal.

The honesty I hoped for was not summoned.

[Later on, I learned from a mutual friend that, despite her other lover's marriage, in her heart and life, it had been I who was the affair.]

Abortion is not easy. The fact that it is a preventable surgical procedure, and surgical procedures are painful and ugly, is only one of several aspects of its agony and hardship.

[Years later, the heart surgery that kept my wise, gentle father-in-law in this world for another decade was painful and ugly. The neck surgery that spared me a lifetime of crippling agony was painful and ugly. The abortion that spared my lover a lifetime of obligation, restraint, and love she felt ill-prepared for was painful and ugly.]

Pregnancy is a pivotal moment. Life-transforming possibilities loom large. Known points of transformational possibility shouldn't be dismissed lightly. It behooves us to regard sexuality and reproduction with reverence.

I didn't (and still don't) believe that what we did was morally wrong. I am uninterested in religious arguments to the contrary.

[What was removed from her body was a part of her body that was growing toward unwanted possibilities. A woman has a right to make the choices that determine her future and health.]

I agreed with my lover's choice, but if I hadn't, I would still have helped her do it, regardless of whether the cells proliferating in her womb were, in fact, my doing.

[The reasons for her choice are a very long story, and much of it is her story to tell, not mine, and would point too clearly to her identity.]

I would agree that at some point in the process of a nine-month gestation, the decision to terminate does, indeed, become a moral choice. From my perspective, the crux of the issue is individuated consciousness, and that cannot be measured or even identified by heartbeat, interpretations of scripture, or the cuteness of tiny toes. It's two-thirds science and one-third intuitive guesswork enhanced with spiritual bias.

[The chicken I ate last week was a sentient being.]

Everyone is or should be on their own with that and a great many other moral choices. With regard to the health, fate, and future of your body, you have a right to be wrong and that's far from liberating.

[Moral ambiguity is the price of consciousness.]

Until the fetus has the possibility of surviving outside the womb, the pregnancy is a medical situation owned entirely by the woman whose body it occupies. Entry into the decision to terminate the pregnancy should be by invitation only, and yes, that exclusion even applies to the "father."

[That exclusion especially applies to wealthy, male politicians.]

What would I have done if she had chosen not to have an abortion? I would have helped. My role would have had to evolve.

[Though a failure in the protocols of contraception seemed more likely in a surreptitious rendezvous than in the more orderly environment of our respective apartments, I thought fatherhood was more a matter of role than genes. Years later, my son would teach me that it's rather more complicated than that.]

The issue of infidelity and paternity would have had to be addressed—not for the sake of genetics scripturalized into romantic superstition, but to dissolve what had become a mutual dishonesty that would poison our relationship by a process as inexorable as gravity.

My unspoken knowledge was an infidelity as deep as her romance with a married man, but I had also been unfaithful in a more conventional sense.

[I was still young enough to be rendered fairly helpless by a pretty woman's desire.]

Marriage? I would have been willing, but that would have almost certainly been a disaster for all, including the child.

[Another long story that is only half mine.]

Music Lessons

Our neighborhood elementary school housed two classrooms, each with two grades. Once weekly, a music teacher came to the school for a joint session with all four grades. The music teacher was a fierce, foolish nerd whose narrow enthusiasm rendered him painfully insensitive. I was in first grade and my brother, Denny, in third, when the music teacher began singling Denny out. He called Denny to the front of the room and ordered him to sing. When my brother was helpless with agonized inhibition, the music teacher berated him in front of the class, while punctuating his words with index finger jabs to the belly. He told him he had a belly like an old man.

When Denny told the story to our father, Clyde asked, "When does he come to your school?"

As the next music class began, the classroom door slammed open. The music teacher's deer in the headlights gaze turned to dismay as Clyde walked in saying, "I thought maybe you'd like to poke this old man in the belly." The teacher backed up to the wall, where Clyde seized the front of his shirt and stood him on tiptoes.

Clyde said, "If you have a problem with my son's behavior, call me and I'll deal with it. But don't you ever lay a hand on him again," and calmly walked out.

Work Ethic

I never liked working for a living.

[I admit that work I could have loved for its intrinsic qualities might have changed all that.]

In fact, I seriously fucking hated it most of the time. From childhood, from before I finished kindergarten, the very idea of fulltime employment filled me with dread. It sounded and later on, as its inexorable necessity commandeered my life, seemed like jail-lite to me.

[I have to accept a difficult-to-assess level of personal responsibility for my failure to find such work. However, the usual practice is that when something is fun, they sell tickets.]

It's not that I thought the world owed me a living—or anything else, for that matter. I didn't feel entitled in the least. Though I regard the mostly profitless enterprises I love as having value far greater than my own amusement, I have no excuses. I felt no need to rationalize or apologize for wanting all the freedom I could get for the unknown, finite span of time fated for this life. It seemed like a raw animal right to me, even when it was clearly wrong in social terms.

[Rights can coexist in conflict. A mama grizzly fearing for the safety of her cubs has every right to tear me apart. I have every right to shoot her to protect my own life. Nature has neither courts nor constitution. It's complicated.]

Tributaries

Back home in the forests of northwestern Pennsylvania after a brief, late winter road trip to southern Texas, I needed to push out into my native terrain deep enough to cleanly feel my physical limits—the rush and push of oxygen and muscle on a steep slope climb and the day's end relaxation of well-worked legs. Bobb's Creek Road (not maintained in winter) was newly clear of the ice packed to its surface by snowmobile use, so I followed it to where both road and stream meet the Tionesta Creek and parked at the school bus turnaround across from Mayburg Bridge.

[Elsewhere, the Tionesta would be called a river.]

I followed Bobb's Creek upstream to the Arner Branch and the Arner upstream to its headwaters, where it became a fast two-foot wide gush of water splashing down a steep-sided gully in a continuous sequence of small waterfalls in dense hemlock shade.

[I liked the Arner Branch because no one else did—it was unremarkable by others' standards and not readily noticed. Its topography of fresh beauty growing over old scars held a gentle healing radiance.]

I craved the space and light of forest on the cusp of spring, so I left the shadowed gully and climbed the short, steep distance to the ridgetop between the Arner and the main branch of Bobb's Creek. I followed the trace of an old logging road out the ridgetop back toward the Tionesta and my truck.

[A sun-bleached deer skull was laying the middle of the fading road/scar. It didn't belong there. I carried it into the woods and placed it facing outward from

the niche formed by two tree roots. Behind it, I left a stone from Texas and in front, a few raisins. Though doing that felt intuitively right, I would have been embarrassed to talk about it.]

On the road's steep descent back to the Arner, my feet went out from under me with a suddenness that obscures the exact cause beyond loose rock and gravity. As I fell backward, I instinctively relaxed into the momentum of the fall in a vain effort to gain control, but the edge of the embankment on the downhill side of the road was at my back—empty space, not solid ground. I did a full, mid-air back flip and landed on my belly three feet below where my boots had been. I was roughed up a bit, but not hurt.

Back in the valley bottom, below the Arner's confluence with Bobb's Creek, I found an access gate to a deer-fenced area enclosing the part of Mayburg that once held houses, a boarding house, school, and church. My maternal grandfather was born there, and his father had lived there most of his life.

[My great grandfather died when I was a child, and I remember him only vaguely as tall, calm, and non-threatening. My more vivid memory is of the high front porch—the house was built on a steep slope—and the large, ornate wood-burning cook stove in the kitchen.]

The buildings had been gone for many years. A few old apple trees, a rusty fire hydrant, and a bottle dump were all that remained of the village. Daffodils and crocuses still rise from the weeds to blossom in the spring.

[Deer tracks and droppings were plentiful inside the deer-proof fence.]

I went inside the gate thinking I would find a place to sit and ponder, but the ambience was oddly poignant in contrast to the sunny day. It was a place of absence now. Sunny days were much more scarce than poignancy in my northwestern Pennsylvania life then, so I walked on.

Bright sunlight glittered on the riffles below Mayburg Bridge, and the sky seemed infinite.

Beyond Compare

I am deeply troubled by the massive scale of human cruelty in relation to the nonhuman world. I also eat meat. I know how to kill, and frankly, it's not that difficult. In the decisive moment, empathy shuts down leaving only fierce purpose at the helm—it's a skill I learned very young.

Though I kill deer without remorse beyond a brief immediate rush of poignancy, a supermarket steak carries a heavy load of cognitive dissonance. Hidden camera films of agribusiness madness make me gasp and weep.

[I try to kill cleanly, but sometimes shit happens.]

When one of my arrows passes through a deer's chest, I'm sure there is a sudden spasm of pain, the magnitude of which I have no means to honestly assess. There is the dizzy choke of lungs no longer able to inflate to receive air, and there is the smell of blood.

[Deer live in a world defined by scent.]

If I do my job with precision, the worst suffering scenario is over in ten to fifteen seconds at most—usually it's quicker than that. Wolves, mountain lions, and coyotes don't kill nearly as gently as a skilled human hunter.

[This comparison is not without meaning, but it neither absolves the human nor condemns the wolf.]

Hunting is a force of nature and though it is no more blameful in itself than magnetism, gravity, or light, compassion is required of conscious beings in proportion to the acuity of their consciousness.

[Otherwise, there is no hope that the world's suffering can be diminished.]

There is a more meaningful comparison to be made: that of a rich, free, natural life ending in a few seconds of panic at the receiving end of one of my arrows compared to a short, miserable lifetime of confinement, knee-deep shit, and sickness ending with a stunning blow to the head followed by semiconscious evisceration.

It's not a matter of killing versus not killing, of a conscious omnivore's ability to become a herbivore. Even vegans kill.

[Consider the multitude of small creatures killed by the machines that harvest grain.]

It's inescapable. Life feeds on life and that is not a choice. The choice we can make is to nurture our compassion by recognizing and embracing the poignancy of sustenance, rather than claiming a godlike right to massive, organized seizures of life. Accepting death's necessity is a very different thing than profaning life itself.

A Hitch in His Get-Along

(for Rollin David Wilson, 1900 – 1971)

Baldy's grandfather was captured by the Confederates at Gettysburg and after a long, hard, hungry march, spent the balance of the war at Andersonville. Baldy's brother returned from World War I with a Silver Star, a Purple Heart, and a broken spirit.

Baldy's father, Scott Wilson, was a blacksmith in Mayburg, Pennsylvania.

[In the mid-twentieth century timber and oil culture of Northwestern Pennsylvania, a widely accepted male ethos of bravado and grace made "outlaw" a colloquial term of cautious admiration for those men who had the wildness of the forest in their blood; they were generous, funny, outrageous, and outspoken men who played hard, drank hard, laughed loudly, poached venison, trusted their luck more than most people dared, and got away with it more than most people thought they deserved. Their surplus energy, which could not be contained by the drudgery of hard labor or the preachings of hellfire and brimstone, nurtured and protected the wildness of the human heart, the wildness that could look into the forest as a mirror and see itself.]

Baldy was an outlaw.

Baldy and a few friends organized Saturday night dances in Mayburg. He was the bouncer. Grizzled characters from lumber camps would come out of the woods looking for booze and a fight, in that order. Baldy's job was to keep them from ruining everyone else's good time. Usually, he could defuse cabin fever and moonshine weirdness with humor and empathy.

One night, a burly character with a reputation for his love of a good brawl arrived fresh from weeks of lumber camp isolation and began harassing people outside. A crowd gathered to watch the seemingly inevitable fight. When Baldy was alerted, he went out, approached the irate drunk from behind, grabbed him by the seat of the pants and shirt collar, lifted him over his head, and threw him completely over a nearby truck. He turned to the fight-hungry spectators and said, "Where's that big son-of-a-bitch everyone was complaining about?"

When Wilda Deshner's passion for Baldy's wild heart culminated in pregnancy, they married. Given the cultural context, their romance must have been powerful, but its story was erased by stigma. Wilda was driven into the crippled spirituality of fundamentalist Methodism by shame and the dominance of self-righteous and unattractive sisters.

[Baldy stood by his commitment to the end of his days, but, like the multiple dimensions of quantum physics, they occupied different worlds in the same space.]

Baldy had driven the train from Mayburg to Sheffield when he learned that Wilda was in labor. He decided to make the return trip, even though there was an ice jam in progress on the Tionesta Creek.

[The Tionesta Creek is larger than many rivers.]

He drove the locomotive as fast as he dared in the strange silver half-light of a New Year's full moon with the rising ice closing over the tracks in the visible distance behind him as he raced down the creekside.

In the depths of the Great Depression, Baldy and a couple of his friends decided, since it was strawberry season when venison is prime, they ought to get some. Home brew probably played a role. They jacklighted a nice fat doe—she went down in her tracks. While one of his friends held the light, Baldy stepped astride the fallen deer. Mysteriously revived, she stood up. The light was dropped and, while his friends were helpless with laughter, he rode the deer off into the darkness.

Baldy knew how to be happy. He was a big-hearted man with a full compliment of the flaws we associate with big-hearted men. While his wife's pious family spewed repression and damnation, he danced in the background and taught his children and grandchildren to laugh and fish.

Baldy drove his car off the bridge that spans the Tionesta at Mayburg. The car landed on one of the concrete supports and hung there, teetering precariously. A bystander heard a voice yell out, "Jesus Christ, the moon's upside down!"

In the fall of 1941, Clyde Darling, the man who would become my father on the far end of that immense decade, was enjoying an after-work beer when Wade and Ira came into the bar, already crazy drunk.

Wade and Ira were bad boys. They lived and worked in lumber camps, often for several weeks at a stretch, then came into town to drink and brawl until their money was gone. The bartender wasn't happy to see them, but feared refusing to serve them would ignite the brawl he wished to avoid. He turned to the men seated at the bar and said, "Drinks on the house for the rest of the night, if anyone can get those two assholes out of here without busting the place up." A tall, wiry man rose from his barstool, walked up behind Wade, grabbed him by the belt and collar, and threw him through the screen door. Ira rushed to his brother's defense and was knocked senseless by a single punch. The man grabbed the semiconscious Ira by the ankles, dragged him outside through the ruined screen door, and dipped Ira's head in the cesspool.

After the man returned to his seat amidst laughter and handshakes, Clyde raised his free beer in a toast to Baldy Wilson. Though he didn't know it at the time, this was Clyde's first encounter with his future father-in-law.

When Mayburg became a ghost town with the closing of the Mayburg Chemical Company in 1943, Baldy and Wilda moved to Warren, and Baldy went to work in a factory that made steel components for a variety of large weapons. One of his duties was to don an asbestos suit, cover his nose and mouth with a wet towel, and enter an idle blast furnace to scrape encrusted debris from its interior walls. They worked in teams a rushed few minutes at a time to avoid the risk of lung damage from the intense heat. Part of their job involved unbolting and replacing large metal plates, and one day in the rush to finish and get back out, they bolted Baldy's thumb down. There was no time for hesitation—he drew his knife and cut his thumb off. Even that small delay scorched his lungs.

[My grandfather never truly recovered from the incident. He healed well at first, but he got old quickly. He must have felt the loss of his vigor keenly, but he

didn't complain. He became wise and his wisdom commingled with his wildness in the same way his former physical vitality had.]

No longer able to hunt, Baldy became the cook (and conversationalist) at Aunt Gert's camp in deer season. When he said, "I just make a big pot of Mulligan," I asked what "Mulligan" was.

"I make a stew with pretty much everything we've got. I keep it on the stove and add stuff to it as it gets eaten. When it turns green, I throw it away and start a new batch."

Reminiscing about a time many years before, when one of his children had been bullied, Baldy said, "I went and had a talk with the boy."

"What did you say?"

"I told him the next time I needed to have a talk with him, I was gonna spike his pecker to a stump and push him over backward." He laughed softly and shook his head.

Baldy said, "This is a special truck—with it, I don't have to pay any attention to speed limits."

"Why is that?"

"Because I have limited speed."

[Baldy was a one-man counterculture within the family. His humor and recklessness—the lightness of his heart—kept the family's ancestral wildness from suffocating beneath the terrible weight of plastic industrial culture.]

Baldy drove a succession of battered old jalopies—hundred-dollar vehicles that only needed to get him around town and trout fishing now and then. After his old truck finally died, his mobility was compromised for a while, until he found a baby-shit brown Volkswagen, which had most definitely seen better days.

That summer, Baldy was late for a family gathering. Just when my aunts, uncles, and parents were beginning to worry, he drove into the yard. Branches, leaves and ferns were stuck in the Volkswagen's windows, doors, trunk lid, and bumpers, making it look like he had driven wildly through a clearcut jungle. He got out of the car wearing one of those novelty fake arrows that give the appearance of one's head being transfixed, danced a little jig, and said, "I was ambushed!" The glove compartment was stuffed with crumpled, wadded currency. He'd had a great afternoon betting on (illegal) cockfights.

[Everyone, except my grandmother, including his grandchildren and great grandchildren, called him "Baldy."]

My mother lamented the misery and injustice of a late April snowstorm.

"It could be worse," Baldy said.

"How?" she asked with audible annoyance leaking from the edges of her voice.

"It could rain cow shit and rocks to splash it," he replied.

[Such humor may have been my first conscious appreciation of multilayered meanings as he separated my mother's complaint from her self-pity, affirmed the validity of the complaint, and substituted laughter and irony for lamentation.]

Clyde and Baldy were talking about a local politician whom they both loathed, probably for a good reason—I don't recall the background or even whether I ever knew it. Clyde launched into a loud rant of manly rage sprinkled with threats of violence. When he paused, Baldy said, "He isn't worthy of a fist, but I'd be happy to slap him until he pissed like a pup," and laughed softly.

Advice from my grandfather seldom came in direct form, rather it was the subtext in stories, so when it emerged from the subtext into direct statement, it commanded attention. Once he told me about a man whose dishonesty had gotten him into a world of trouble.

"He didn't intend to be that way. He only meant to tell one small lie, but every lie needs seven more to make it stick. That's why it only takes one lie to make a liar of you."

I was sitting beside Baldy at Mayburg Old Home Day. His morbidly obese, fundamentalist sister-in-law, Lottie, walked past.

[Lottie and her sister, Helen, were ever eager to forthrightly assure anyone and everyone that if you drank beer or failed to attend the right church regularly, you were doomed to eternal hellfire.]

"She'll grow a lot of nice flowers on her grave when she dies," he said.

"Why is that?"

"Lotta shit there."

I showed Baldy an odd-shaped machine part I had found in the woods near Mayburg and asked, "What do you suppose this was for?"

"It looks like a hooty-cackle for on the butt end of a sneeze bar," he replied.

My girlfriend and I were making love on my parents' living room floor when the front door opened, and Baldy walked in. Seeming to take no notice, he walked past us, through the dining room, into the kitchen, and closed the kitchen door behind him. We heard the refrigerator open and close, a can of beer being opened, and the back door open and close.

As Baldy's emphysema progressed, he could barely cross a room without pausing to catch his breath, but he refused to give up trout fishing. He loved to fish little forest streams for native brook trout with a long fly rod, a bait casting reel, and night crawlers. He walked miles into the woods in twenty-foot increments. His daughters (my mother and aunt) were worried.

[His blend of patience and courage was a larger lesson than I understood at the time.]

Aunt Gert asked, "Dad, what are we going to do if you don't come back one of these times?"

"Wait a week or two and take a walk. You'll smell me," he replied.

My plunge into the late-sixties zeitgeist seemed to send seismic shock waves through the boondock Methodist contingent of my mother's family. Some were forthright in their conviction that I had embraced both eternal damnation and present treason, while others were content to merely squirm and fill the room with the veiled vibes of their nervous confusion.

My grandfather mostly seemed not to notice, but one day, as we drank my father's beer while he was at work, Baldy said, "You know back in Prohibition, me and my friends used to buy illegal booze knowing that some of the bad stuff out there could make you go blind or worse, but we knew each other and knew who we could trust. Make sure you know who you can trust."

I said, "That's what life is all about."

We tapped our bottles in a toast.

Following a tip from my grandfather, I went to Hank's Plumbing to apply for a job as a clerk/shop assistant/laborer.

"So you're looking for a job, huh? Well, come on, let's go out back," Hank said, as he picked up a softball and walked out the back door. I followed. In the backyard, he gestured to where he wanted me to go twenty-five feet away and threw the softball at me—hard.

I have an eye convergence problem, which compromises my depth perception. In order to make the catch I had to get my face directly in front of the ball and save myself with my right hand. So, that's what I did. I caught the ball and fired it right back at his face.

He caught it and asked, "Why are you out of work now?" as he threw the ball again. I caught it, threw it back, and said, "I dropped out of college."

He threw the ball back, "Why?"

"School didn't seem nearly so attractive after I flunked my draft physical."

Hank caught and returned the ball, "Why'd they flunk you."

I caught and returned, "I don't have binocular vision—shitty depth perception—it's no big deal."

[This was a lie. I had evaded the draft by claiming to harbor "homosexual tendencies" and catching a hard thrown ball was, indeed, a big deal.]

He caught the ball and threw it back hard, "When can you start?"

"Right now," I said and tossed the ball to him gently.

"What's with the beard?"

"Nothing, it just grew there all by itself."

Hank laughed and said, "Yeah, I guess so."

I spent the rest of the day learning Hank's bookkeeping method, how to operate the pipe threading machine, how to handle sales, and getting an introduction to Hank's collection of pornographic magazines.

I bought a 1963 Rambler station wagon for a hundred thirty-five dollars.

Baldy was hospitalized when the emphysema that had been steadily draining his vitality for years reached its final, critical stage. It was obvious to all that death was closing in on him fast.

Aunt Gert said tearfully, "Dad, don't leave us."

"Do I look like I'm going anywhere?"

A nurse brought his dinner.

Baldy turned to me and said. "This hospital food makes me wish I was a dog."

"Why is that?"

"So I could lick my ass and get the taste out of my mouth."

He died the next day.

My parents moved to North Carolina not long after Baldy died. I lingered in northwest Pennsylvania for a while and dreamed of wild, faraway possibilities.

[He was so intensely alive, even when he was half-dead, that mourning seemed unnatural, and my journey from grief to gratitude was short. The

wisdom beneath the surface of his wildness slowly bubbled to the surface in the decades after he was gone.]

From my earliest memory, my grandmother had parakeets. They all had names, but no one ever spoke about them. They were just there, one or two at a time, in a cage in the dining room.

There were no more birds after Baldy died.

My parents had expressed a longing to have a dog again, and their new home in North Carolina had a large fenced-in yard. They also wanted me to visit them before I headed for the West Coast. On the way, I stopped to visit my friend and former teacher, Aaron, and traded a selection of my prints for a Borzoi puppy, Mona.

[Aaron bred and raised Borzois, some of whom seemed like canine bodhisattvas.]

As I traveled southward, it became obvious that my aging Rambler's top speed was in steady decline. A mechanic told me it would take two days and more money than the car was worth to resurrect it. Creeping into West Virginia at thirty-five mph with the gas pedal to the floor, a change of strategy was called for. I checked into a motel and dropped off Mona and my worldly belongings. Then, I drove to a supermarket parking lot a half-mile away, scraped off the inspection sticker, removed the license plate, and walked back to the motel. On the way, I bought two cheeseburgers—one for Mona and one for me. I called my parents and explained the delay in my expected arrival.

The next morning, I stuck out my thumb with a knapsack, two large bags, and a puppy. My mother picked me up not far down the road. My father was utterly smitten with Mona.

My parents paid for an airplane ticket to San Francisco. I didn't have a place to settle, but I had a phone number for a bright friend who was living in a commune in Oakland.

Food Stamps

A friend's father visiting his son for a day offered to loan Jack (my apartment mate) and me his car for grocery shopping. The end of the fall semester was approaching. December's half-month of parental feeding gave new abundance to our monthly food stamp allotment—it was party time. We drove Brian's father's car to the large supermarket just outside of town to buy things like pineapples, whole watermelons, artichoke hearts, and steaks in addition to brown rice, soy sauce, oatmeal, and green beans. We paid for the contents of our two overloaded shopping carts with food stamps, loaded it into our borrowed, brand new, white Cadillac, and drove away.

That Old-Time Religion

The various words and names used to render deity a thing to be spoken of (God, Allah, Jehovah, Jayzus!, Atman, The Great Pumpkin, et al) are so freighted with disparate meanings and cover so many possibilities of interpretation as to be (functionally) nearly meaningless. That's why so many people, especially those who already harbor too many strange voids within, feel compelled to personalize it—to give it not only a name, but often a face, a personality, even a gender.

[I confess that I don't understand the heartfelt urgency of their need. I've never felt it. My heart has been broken many times by both certainties and doubts, but never by mystery.]

Though comforting illusions can seem sweetly benign, when great mysteries are synthetically concretized they encourage narrow-mindedness and diminish compassion.

[Human violence didn't come from Pleistocene carnivorousness; it came from the angry gods of tyrannical myth. It came from the civilized savagery of punished children.]

I find most vocal prayers (forgivably) embarrassing. It seldom seems to occur to the perpetrators that their prideful proclamations of humility and gratitude offered up as barter for divine favors might be socially awkward for persons too honest to bow their heads and mutter in a camouflage charade.

[Generally speaking, supplication is unhealthy, though it is certainly understandable if you're down and bleeding. It's not good to have a beggared

relationship with a person, god, or nature. The human spirit is not improved by groveling, and wounded pride is a poor substitute for humility.]

Though I am one of those who gaze unbowed either distractedly ahead or furtively about the room hoping the display of piety will be brief; even when the merciful brevity is not granted, I silently endure and forgive. But still, life and love fully provide plenty of sad sighs without help from the rude presumptuousness of Christian displays of voodoo-lite.

My refusal to bow my head and pretend is neither prideful nor defiant (well, maybe it's a little defiant); I just can't fucking do it.

[Inhibition and honesty become allies in the absence of desire.]

If I were a more patient man, the inability of believers to understand the difference between disbelief and nonbelief would be less vexing.

[Though ritual and ceremony savored deeply, but held lightly, can be at least therapeutic and often more, a person who thinks they can change reality with magical incantations is delusional. There are better things to aspire to than becoming some sort of minor league Merlin. Demeaning the intrinsic wonder of conscious attention with fantasies of magic will lead away from possibilities of transcendence, not toward them.]

The real value of religion is simply as a means to nurture an affectionate reciprocal relationship with reality. An affectionate reciprocal relationship with reality is a sound foundation for unconditional kindness.

[Religion isn't the only way to have such a relationship with reality, but it works well for many people across a broad spectrum of intelligence, talent, and education. The downside is that it is easily weaponized by demagogues.]

When religion oversteps the bounds of this fundamental purpose, the result is rather like intestinal contents leaking into the abdominal cavity—there is a deadly, raging infection. Seriously ugly shitloads of anger fester into self-destructive fevers of violence and stupidity. This often results in cruel fools invested with great power and atrocities committed (or at least financed) by people whose hearts are fundamentally kind.

*[Dogma doesn't merely encourage violence; it **is** violence.]*

There are times of inner clarity manifest in outward perceptions (mostly in encounters with art, nature, and loving sex) when I seem to be witnessing the divine at work in the world.

[The above is a descriptive statement, not a prescriptive one.]

Both divinity and soul are necessary components of my expressive vocabulary. To arbitrarily constrain either with particularities of belief seems arrogant, presumptuous, and irreverent.

[Namaste.]

Field Work

My job was weird, dull, crazy, mostly pointless, and sometimes ugly, but that hardly mattered.

[I was a caseworker with the Warren County office of the Pennsylvania Department of Public Welfare.]

Getting out of the city mattered. My time in Chicago had been an almost yearlong spasm of dirt and dysfunction redeemed only by the art museum and the university library.

Now, I could drink beer and smoke weed by campfires, go for daylong hikes on weekends, and buy acrylic paint by the pint, stretchers by the dozen, and canvas in twenty-yard rolls.

[I painted five to seven hours daily.]

My understanding of color was honing itself to a razor's edge. Shapes were evolving through long sequences of incremental change, taking on new meanings while retaining traces of old ones, until their psychological resonance became deeply layered and nuanced. Whatever the outward, critical, objective value of my work, it was clearly taking me into psychological and intellectual realms I had previously been transported to only through the works of chemically-enhanced friends and famous others.

[Making art seemed like enough, at least as long as I didn't slack off and lose my momentum. Painting was a revelation in slow motion. I lived for it. I

lived in it. Happiness, in any conventional sense, was not a particularly relevant factor; I didn't allow it to be. First, I needed to redeem myself, to myself.]

A committee was appointed to simplify Pennsylvania's application process for welfare, Medicaid, and food stamps. Until then, the application form filled both sides of a single sheet of paper, with space for changes, notes, and new signatures at each quarterly, six month, or annual eligibility review, depending on the type of case. With the new, "simplified" process, a six-page application form had to be completed from scratch, in the client's presence, with each regular eligibility review. It was a painstaking process that could be downright harrowing if the client was coughing and hacking with the flu, hadn't bathed in months, there were chickens scurrying and fluttering around the kitchen catching and eating cockroaches, and/or the house was littered with dog shit and rotting garbage.

[Kitchens were best for interviews because they tended to have hard chairs. Sitting on stuffed furniture was often inadvisable.]

The first time I had to complete one of the new forms on a home visit was with an unwashed, dull-eyed young couple from a family for whom the Great Depression had never ended. It took forty-five minutes to complete the form, meticulously asking even those questions I already knew the answers to. They both squirmed and fidgeted constantly throughout the interview. Finally, as they signed the completed application, the woman said, "We went to the doctor yesterday. He said we have scabies."

I drove home, stuffed all my clothes in the washer, and took a very hot shower. For weeks afterward, an itch would trigger a momentary spasm of panic and revulsion.

***January 26, 1977:** Snow.*
Kirk's birthday.
Pancakes.
Office.
TK shuffles by in his polyester leisure suit.
Distraught clients on the phone—a blizzard is coming and they haven't enough fuel oil and no money—shivering people and freezing pipes. Agway won't deliver without money up front. I give them a bullshit mini-speech about an emergency program that is (theoretically) going to be implemented soon, etcetera. They know I'm just trying to get them off the phone as painlessly as possible.

I made phone calls, even though I didn't have much hope. I argued with Agway, even though it was pure pretense. My "Sorry, I tried" phone call was well rehearsed and smoothly delivered.

The blizzard rolled in and everything shut down, including the welfare office. By two-thirty, I was home stretching canvases and getting high.

Evening painting was halted by a welcome interruption—Terry, alone and radiant. An hour of small rambling talk and a cascade of kisses flowed from the studio to the bedroom.

I rose from warm afterglow to dress and walk her home and get high with her husband.

I realize that I'm a real asshole.

Back home, I began and finished a three-foot square canvas filled with bright yellows and iridescent gold and titled it "Terry's Light."

And wrote these words in the wee hours.

The day's first interview was a young single mother who had fled from a town forty miles away to escape her abusive boyfriend. She said the car was in her name, but her boyfriend had been the main person who drove it. Since she fled abruptly with few possessions, she hadn't looked in her trunk until she arrived in Warren. There was something in the trunk that worried her, though she wasn't sure what it was. She asked if I would take a look at it, so after the interview, I accompanied her to her car. The worrisome item was a bazooka. I brought her back to the office and called the police.

January 31, 1977: *I still have people freezing and fuel suppliers behaving like archetypal capitalist pigs.*

Still no fuel oil for the L family. A neighbor gave them a couple of five-gallon cans. Mounds of bureaucratic shit. Busy signals, tape-recorded messages, and, "I'm sorry, but I don't have the authority to...," and "Mr. L applied for a credit card and was rejected." Goddamned corporate motherfuckers—but I stay cool, think of five o'clock, walking home, river ducks, painting, smoke, Terry's touch...

At four-fifty, I make one last phone call and I've got the L family a hundred gallons of fuel oil.

I made a home visit to review Medicaid and food stamp eligibility. The house was incredibly filthy. An old woman bedridden after several strokes, joints swollen with arthritis, twitched one arm up and down, gasping for breath and mumbling in an eastern European language. Her dim daughter had the wood stove so stoked that the heat and stench were stifling. I felt numb.

February 1, 1977: The morning staff meeting was filled with verbal flatulence about the "energy crisis." Token efforts proposed with deep sincerity while carefully dodging away from the simple, ancient moral imperative of keeping everyone, the whole fucking tribe, warm and fed through the winter. We, of course, as the Department of Public Welfare, lack the power to do it, though if we had that power (money) we could actually do it pretty easily. Keep everyone warm and fed. Take care of the sick and wounded. Civilization 101.

I went to lunch with TK. First we took a short drive to smoke a joint—he had to move his car to avoid a parking ticket, anyway—then we went to a bar two blocks from the office. TK washed down his Elavil with a gin and tonic and ordered another round. I ordered a Wild Turkey and a cheeseburger.

Not long after we returned to the office, I finished a phone call with a difficult client and glanced toward TK's desk. He was facedown, snoring softly, with a lit cigarette in each hand. I extinguished his cigarettes and tapped his shoulder.

"Are you okay, man?"

"Yeah, I just didn't sleep well last night."

February 21, 1977: Sketch and paint.
Books, tea, and bagels.
Secretly half-waiting for Terry's hoped-for door tap.
Happy, blue-skied windows.
And the door tap comes…
She is so different from me—so young, such a different life…why does she feel so right, good, and fated in my arms? What can we be to each other?

The family had lived for generations in an old farmhouse without inside plumbing. Sometime in the 1950s the privy filled up. No one in the household was sufficiently sober or competent to build a new one.

The house had the typical floor plan of an old farmhouse. Off to one side of the front door there was a parlor that in older times would have been the room with nice furniture, where one entertained the preacher on Sunday afternoon. The parlor was empty and unused, so they cut a hole in the floor and shat into the basement for twenty years. The case narrative warned caseworkers not to visit during the summer.

February 22, 1977: *Night truck growl.*
Furnace hum.
A strand of Terry's hair on my desk.
Spring-like warmth.
Crescent moon through broken clouds.
And the late writing of this against the coming sleep. (Time slides stealthily.)

The apartment was threadbare, but tidy, which was a pleasant surprise because the young, single mother I was there to interview came from a family of notorious dirt and dysfunction. She was washing dishes as I asked questions and took notes. A puppy scampered into the room and pissed on the floor. She wiped up the urine with the dishcloth and went back to washing dishes with it.

March 1, 1977: *Most nights, I paint later than I intend to—often oversleep, hurry to the office, and yawn through the workday morning. For a while, I thought I was simply disorganized, but lately I've realized that it is often in defenseless moments of fatigue that ideas and images break loose from the depths and float to the surface. The mental second wind I get after struggling to stay awake is a time of special clarity—often the best time to begin a new painting. Though I pay a price for that clarity, not only in tired mornings, but also in emotional fragility, for now, living without it seems like it would be a lot harder than paying its price.*

Robert was a fellow caseworker whose quick, sarcastic wit sometimes sparkled darkly, but his attitude was beyond bad.
[He once signed a letter informing a client that they would be prosecuted for welfare fraud, "Love, Bobbie."]
Robert's knee-jerk loathing of authority was rendered aggressive by a heavy dose of short man's syndrome, and led him into constant antagonism with management. He staged confrontations on the flimsiest pretexts and openly bragged of his intention to drive the director out of his job.
[The director carried his own heavy array of quirks and dysfunctions and commanded little respect from his staff, but like me and most, he was just trying to navigate through his workdays with a minimum of headaches and enough leftover energy for a life. Though, at times, he was carelessly unfair in small ways, if you treated your colleagues with a modicum of respect, and your work was good enough to slide through an audit relatively unscathed, you would be

subject to little scrutiny and could steal small nuggets of freedom for whatever freedom meant to you.]

Part of the problem with Robert was that, in his first months on the job, he had behaved more cautiously, and the director, whom he now bitterly referred to as a "dictator," had allowed him to stay long enough to gain permanent civil service status, instead of firing him while he was still on probation. And then Robert got elected union steward, because the only other candidate was TK, who tended to get drunk on lunch hour, largely because childhood tragedy had chewed his psyche ragged. Now, firing Robert would require far worse transgressions than simply being an argumentative pain-in-the-ass.

[Caseworkers had regularly scheduled field days for conducting case reviews in the clients' homes. We took applications and reviewed ongoing eligibility for welfare, food stamps and Medicaid.]

In mid-morning on my field day, en route to Terry's apartment in the state car, I passed the director en route to the office from his home.

[He was coming to work two hours late.]

We waved to each other as we passed in front of Robert's house, where Robert's car was conspicuously parked in the driveway. It was his field day too.

Terry was alone and her year-old daughter was napping soundly. Our hunger for each other was fresh and urgent, but shedding our clothes and going to bed was way too risky, especially with the constant flow of people through three apartments with overlapping circles of friends and drug deals. We sat on the couch and smoked a joint. Talk flowed into touches, touches into kisses, and the rising fervor of kisses into unbuttoning and unbuckling. I was on the verge of helplessness in the flood of sensation, when the door opened.

[I hate it when that happens.]

A mutual friend walked in, halted in startled embarrassment, turned, and exited.

[There were no repercussions—the friend kept his silence.]

When I returned to the office, the director asked to speak with me in private. He asked if I had seen Robert's car parked in his driveway, and I said that I had, indeed, seen it there.

"Would you be willing to testify to that in a hearing?"

"If I am asked, I will speak the truth."

[The problem with stealing field time using your own car was that you had to turn in mileage reimbursement reports, and that put you in the position of stealing money unless you could fit your personal agenda into artificial spaces built into a genuine field day schedule. With the state car, you had to be sure the miles driven were not flagrantly out of line with the documentable work done,

but this left plenty of latitude, because we often had to track clients down to boondock addresses with poor directions.]

My personal agendas were mostly pretty simple (a nice secluded place in the woods to pull over, get high, write, read, and draw), until Terry came into my life.

[When her husband, Lynn, was laid off, I took their application for Medicaid and arranged for the Commonwealth of Pennsylvania to pay for the birth of their child.]

Terry's apartment was on a dead-end street within my geographically assigned caseload, so the time I stole to be with her involved no stolen money. This wasn't merely an ethical distinction—it was a serious legal issue as well. An hour hanging out with a sketchbook, a trout stream, or a lover was goofing off. Not going out at all and then covering one's tracks with a false mileage expense report was fraud.

[Using small portions of one's field time for personal matters, like paying a bill, going to the post office, picking up a prescription, or cashing a check, etcetera, was a widespread practice and widely regarded as a compensatory perk for the ugliness and squalor we frequently had to wade into. But I also have to admit that I regularly stretched that slack to its elastic limits and beyond.]

Though I had recurring, well-earned spasms of guilt with regard to Terry's husband, who was an honest man, a generous friend, and my primary source of marijuana, I did my job well and got good performance evaluations. Could I have been a better caseworker if I had given the job all of its allotted (and paid) hours? Theoretically, I suppose, but if I had played by the rules, my performance could also very well have been worse. The pressures exerted by my stolen time were a harsher taskmaster than any supervisor, and the strange slack I granted myself had more to do with survival than greed, ego, or lust. One could rationally argue that stealing time was in essence stealing money, but the simple fact remains that I did my job, not excellently, but somewhat more than adequately.

[There's little value in retrospectively finessing my ethics in this regard, because I neither rationalized nor agonized it at the time. I was getting by and I was making art. Getting by is a fulltime job when you have Post Traumatic Stress Disorder and chronic depression. I was desperately in love, even though I would have preferred not to be.]

Robert was fired. The rest of the staff was relieved to see him and the stressed out, combative atmosphere he generated gone. The firing was appealed and upheld. I testified at the appeal hearing.

The hypocrisy of testifying that Robert had abused field time when I had witnessed it while not only abusing field time myself, but doing so to carry on an affair with an eighteen-year old, married former client didn't trouble me.

[Robert was an asshole.]

I hadn't felt so much in a very long time. I had almost forgotten I could. In moments granted by chance, we were drawn into each other's arms by a force as natural and irresistible as wind or the flow of water. Often, we only had time for a tender meeting of eyes and perhaps a kiss. In younger days such occasions might have been so awash in sexual frustration as to dampen my ardor, but now I gratefully received them as undeserved blessings.

One of my clients committed suicide. I liked him and knew he was going to do it. He was trapped in terminal medical misery and had a right to his choice. To say that my colleagues would have found this morally and professionally ambiguous is rather an understatement—it could have gotten me officially disciplined, if not fired. So I didn't talk about it. I carried some guilt, but intervening would have been such a cruel betrayal—his life was painfully and irremediably shrunken, and he trusted me.

March 15, 1977: Library books overdue in Jamestown—calling garages about van repairs.

Sunshine streets.

Hurried walking.

Thoughts of woodland light, leaves, and softness.

Victoria's diagnosis has been changed to schizophrenia. I'm not surprised, but it's sad.

Mark time, chalk up minutes, wait.

Coffee break walk in bright sun.

Drawing.

In late afternoon, the dullness thickens and the background murmur becomes more abstract. Rich's radio muzak—tiny dancer—murmur. (Out, I want out of here!)

Phone calls—scribble notes and adorn them with doodles.

"Blue jean baby, LA lady..."

Call the hospital billing office. The collections clerk isn't in. I'll call back.

"...with me..."

Scribble. Check my calendar. What appointments do I have scheduled tomorrow?

"…hold me closer tiny dancer…"

Telephone. "Will my medical card cover support stockings? The pharmacy wouldn't do it."

"Yes, that's covered. Go back and tell them prior authorization is no longer required. Tell them to call me if they have a problem."

Hang up the phone and re-enter ambient reality. The muzak has taken a turn for the worse. Fucking Donnie Osmond—this is torture!

Painting and pushups tonight.

New changes in employment regulations render enforcement practically impossible. Other caseworkers bitch about it. I nod in seeming agreement and respond with noncommittal, cynical sarcasms. I'm secretly pleased because I've never hassled people about it anyway. I don't care if they want to work or not. If someone really wants to work and there's anything I can do to facilitate that, I'm happy to oblige, but I have better things to do than make people run around to offices and interviews with beer on their breath. Not getting hired is easy. I fill out the forms and keep quiet. What most people call ambition mostly seems like another form of sloth to me.

Road kills melting out of the snow banks.

The interior of the client's house was a foot deep in garbage. Narrow, trodden-down pathways wended through every room. In the living room a vacuum cleaner stood, half buried. It was plugged in.

On a cold wet spring evening, I took a break from painting to walk four blocks in drizzling rain to Lynn and Terry's apartment.

[I was strangely addicted to the ache of my longing.]

Lynn's father, Clair, stopped by. He politely ignored the heavy scent of freshly smoked marijuana. I was a few years older than the others and had professional experience sufficiently parallel to Clair's (state government bureaucracy) to give us a degree of common ground that he was surprised to find among his son's hippie friends. The sly humor and slightly cruel ironies of his conversation displayed a level of verbal sophistication that was too rare in my life in small town Pennsylvania. In the background, I also knew that he had been a rather worse than merely inadequate father to Lynn, whose psychic wounds from his father's multiple stormy marriages were more visible than he was willing to admit to himself.

When I rose from my chair to leave (the studio beckoned), Clair said he needed to be on his way as well and offered me a ride home, which I gratefully accepted. When we pulled up in front of my apartment, Clair told me how very much he had enjoyed our conversation and fished heavy-handedly for an invitation. He was making a more than obvious pass at me. I begged off with gentle excuses.

The world's strangeness seemed a deep and sad companion as I painted far into the night.

Shit

In territory we preferred not to speak of in the presence of adults, across the railroad tracks, behind a construction company, there was a brushy field littered with debris from the construction and demolition of buildings: lumber scraps, pieces of plywood, cement blocks, bricks, cable, corrugated metal, sluice pipes, and large weathered stacks of lumber.

One summer, my brother, Denny, a few friends, and I disassembled and reassembled a cabin-sized junk pile into what still looked like a junk pile, but had a secret entrance covered by a sheet of corrugated metal and secured with cement blocks. Inside, low narrow passageways connected several small rooms. We labored extraordinarily hard, and there were casualties—I smashed the tip of my thumb so badly it split open, and Denny stepped on a nail, necessitating a trip to the emergency room and a tetanus shot.

Our secret hideaway was filled with adventurous fantasies and dark, wonderful secrecy, until a dim-bulb ruffian (our age, but not part of our circle of friends) discovered the hidden entrance and took a shit in the main room. He lacked sufficient luck to offset his lack of stealth, and we caught him as he exited. We forced him back in, sealed the entrance with many cement blocks and two by fours, and left him there for most of the hot summer day. When we freed him, he crawled out gasping and weeping, and our shame had more to do with the subsequent abandonment of our hideaway than with the pile of excrement inside.

Boots of Appalachian Rubber

One of the first times my son was able to go for a hike and carry his own small knapsack (with an extra layer of clothing and some food); we stopped for lunch where a weathered fallen log looked like a perfect bench. When we gathered our things to walk on, I told him to leave his apple core on a stump because a chipmunk or squirrel would find it and feel like it was Christmas morning. That thought summoned delighted laughter, and on future hikes, he always brought offerings of food for the animals: an apple, a handful of nuts and raisins, or a few sunflower seeds.

Our subsequent conversations about reciprocity (yes, at age four) renewed my awareness of my own largely unmet need to give something back to the forest and its creatures for all they gave to us and that we took from them.

[Children teach us gently by summoning us to listen to our own wisdom.]

Most of our hiking, hunting, and fishing in those days took place in the valley of the North Fork of Six Mile Run, a (then) pristine trout stream in the Allegheny National Forest on the northern fringes of Appalachia.

[It is now an oil field with "No Trespassing" signs.]

The North Fork fed us. We ate its squirrels, grouse, rabbits, trout, blueberries, fiddleheads, blackberries, and apples. But it was the deer that really made a difference in our diet, budget, and the meaning of home. They were our umbilical to the North Fork and to the wild Earth. They roamed that land, sampled nearly all its plant life, and concentrated it in their muscles. And we distilled it further into our bodies. The deer of the North Fork lived in our very bones.

[A working hypothesis: the karmic redemption required by the death that feeds us is only found by living well in the truth of wildness and compassion.]

That fall's mast crop was poor, and the winter that followed was harsh. The deer were visibly thin by winter's end. I found the remains of a young doe who had stood on her hind legs in an effort to eat out-of-reach browse. She slipped and wedged a front leg into the tight v of the tree's double trunk. She had struggled fiercely and hung there until she died.

Deer often suffer from serious vitamin and mineral deficiencies toward the end of even a mild winter. Their hardest time isn't during the fierce cold of January, but during March when most of the available food has been eaten and new growth hasn't yet risen. Their nutritional deficit has to be caught up quickly to enable the growth of unborn fawns and antlers. So, early that spring as the snow melted off, I bought a thirty-five pound vitamin and mineral supplement block, crammed it into my daypack, and headed for the North Fork.

Rushing snowmelt had swept away the fallen hemlock that had been my bridge across the creek for several years. A short distance upstream, I found a newly fallen yellow birch that looked a little on the small side, but possible. Halfway across, the log shifted. After a few seconds of frantic ballet, I thought I was going to make it, but just as that thought arose, I was airborne. I landed on my back in shockingly cold water. But I was still fully prepared to laugh until the rushing creek water poured into the open top of my backpack, which couldn't be closed due to the size and shape of the vitamin and mineral block. In the current, the block was an anchor and the pack was a sail.

The realization that I was about to be swept into deeper water beneath an undercut bank unleashed an electric jolt of fear and a flood of adrenaline. I reached across my chest with my right hand, grabbed the left pack strap, and tore it completely off the backpack. It seemed to offer no more resistance than if it had been made of paper, but as the day passed, my hand and wrist swelled and throbbed. Every tendon and ligament had been stretched farther than they were meant to stretch.

Nevertheless, I carried my offering up the ridge to a small, open area where several deer trails converged. The fire I built only temporarily eased the bone-deep chill because I didn't build it big enough or linger long enough to fully dry my clothes. I knew, on the way out, I would simply wade the swollen creek and hurry home to a hot bath, whisky, and my wife.

Soaking in our old, enameled iron, claw-foot bathtub, I remembered when my father was first able to buy good, warm leather hunting boots, not only for himself (he would never have bought them only for himself), but for his sons as well. The cheap, not-so-warm rubber muck boots of poorer times were permanently banished. It was a grand indulgence and a point of pride nearly as great as his ability to buy a brand-new car. Good boots were important. The comfort of well-oiled, form-fitting leather was a symbol of his hard-earned success.

[For my father, rubber boots were a symbol of poverty and ignorance, of horseshit and bad memories.]

A week later, liberated from inherited prejudice by shock and risk, I bought a pair of good, insulated rubber boots. I reveled in my newfound ability to wade small creeks with ease on my unplanned wandering hikes—a capability that became precious when corporate oil-lust devoured the North Fork, and I had to seek new territory for sustenance and wandering.

Searching out new, relatively unwounded wild land became two decades of wonderful exploration of the land of my ancestors, just in time for a glimpse of what it could have been without oil.

[A gift of cold water and rubber boots.]

The Sacred and the Obscene

I was raised as a Free Methodist—kind of—that was the church we attended, my maternal grandmother's church, but my parents never talked about religion. Presented without passion, the mythic stories didn't stick, didn't ring true, even to an eight-year old. The well-meaning people at the church didn't seem smart enough to command the significance they claimed.

[As an adult, I've come to rely on more rigorous and, I hope, less arrogant ways of thinking.]

In 1967, I began college well read in philosophy, but knowing little of substance about the religion I grew up in or any others. When the countercultural zeitgeist of the late sixties swept into northwestern Pennsylvania, I was one of those eagerly swept up. It was in the antiwar movement that I first encountered Catholicism up close and personal, in the form of Father Z, the priest assigned to minister to the religious needs of students at Clarion State College (now Clarion University of Pennsylvania). He and his gentle Methodist counterpart opened a coffee house in the Campus Ministry, across an alley from the Catholic Church. The Campus Ministry became a hub for the better-behaved factions of the anti-war movement and the hippie community.

In his office, Father Z had a high-quality stereo system and an amazing record collection. He drove a hot black Mustang that seemed stunningly cool, even though it would have commanded much less respect driven by a wealthy student. In Father Z, I encountered deep faith and conviction perfectly wedded to gentleness and compassion. His office was a safe haven for broken hearts, bad trips, and the lonely confusions of rampant hormones in wildly changing times.

No matter how fucked-up you were or why, Father Z would offer shelter, safety, sympathy, and perhaps a bit of gentle advice, but never judgment, lecture, moral superiority, or dominance. He was not without a certain vanity—he knew he was cool—but not even his vanity was entangled in his ego. The situation was always about you, not him. Father Z's loving kindness often brought a seeming naiveté to his gentle words, demeanor, and smile, but there was also a tougher, harder truth in his eyes.

When I told him about my dawning engagement with Buddhism, he said, "I am wholly committed to Christianity, but I think Buddhism will lead you closer to God, not farther away."

[My great aunt assured me that I would burn in Hell.]

My sojourn among the better behaved was short-lived, but Father Z and I stayed in touch.

Father Z was gay. I never witnessed anything overt to justify that assertion beyond his visible comfort among a circle of gay friends, but I would, without hesitation, bet the farm on it. Was he perfectly celibate? Probably not, but I think he deserves the same non-judgmental compassion he so freely gave. There was one close friendship that almost certainly crossed the line before it evolved into something else, but it did indeed evolve into something else. They were there for each other as friends during some very hard times including the aneurysm that eventually killed Alan. Father Z taught valuable lessons even in his lapses, and that was in itself a lesson of inestimable value that grew through years of evolving awareness.

[I have always assumed that celibates stray from celibacy at a rate similar to that at which spouses stray from fidelity in marriage. Both failings are similarly wrong and eminently forgivable to the degree that they are not chronic and repetitive.]

A decade after I left Clarion, my wife and I were married in a civil ceremony. Three and a half years later, we decided to marry again in the Catholic Church, mainly for the benefit of my devout father-in-law. Since Terry's first marriage had also been a civil ceremony, getting the necessary annulment from the church was largely a paperwork formality. But we were required to attend counseling sessions with Father Finucan, an earthy, good-humored Irish priest.

Not far into our first session," Father Finucan said, "Now there's the issue of raising your children in the Catholic Church."

"I'm a Buddhist, and when my son asks questions, he's going to get Buddhist answers."

"But will he be exposed to the church and its teachings?"

"Oh yes, I have thirty undergraduate credits in philosophy and Terry's father is very active in the church. We want our son to understand his heritage and be exposed to all the major religions."

"Then don't worry about it—this is just shit left over from the Inquisition."

That broke the ice and the rest of the interview was both casual and frank. Father Finucan's clear intention was to facilitate our marriage within the Church, not to obstruct it or pound its square peg into a round hole. As soon as the annulment was official, we scheduled a wedding with Father Finucan.

Since my openness to the Church, beyond my desire to please my father-in-law, was largely due to my friendship with Father Z, I asked him to be our best man.

The wedding was small—we invited only parents, siblings, and my grandmother, who believed Catholics were doomed to hellfire and damnation, but whose kindness to all was impeccable. When Father Finucan began the ceremony, he noticed Father Z sitting next to Terry's parents and stopped.

"Sam, what are you doing here?"

"I'm the best man."

"Well, you know these folks better than I do—you should marry them."

Father Z laughed softly and traded places with Father Finucan. We were married by our best man.

In the years that followed, I had many long, late, sometimes wine-fueled conversations with my father-in-law, John about our respective beliefs. Within John's large Irish family, I attended Catholic weddings and funerals and I admired both the openness and informality of the Church's human side and the formal rigor and devotion of its ceremonies. Both stood in sharp contrast with the harsh judgments and dull procedural ceremonies I had endured as a child. I thought that if I were ever to become a Christian, I would be a Catholic.

[My ever becoming a Christian was beyond unlikely. I was a Buddhist even before I knew what to call my beliefs.]

The gentle goodness of heart I saw in Father Z and John became the face of the Catholic Church in my life and was strong enough to outweigh broader opinions about organized religion and the absurdities of theology. I also knew that they both had their own disagreements with Church policies and politics, but saw divine goodness at the core of its unending process of evolution, regardless of what happened out on its ragged human fringes. That's how my relationship with Catholicism remained for more than three decades—an affectionate truce.

In the early nineties, as a casework supervisor for the Pennsylvania Department of Public Welfare (DPW), I was the liaison between DPW and all nongovernmental charities serving Warren County. My job was to coordinate services to ensure that no organization expended its resources on needs better met by another agency or program, that services were not wastefully duplicated, and needs that DPW couldn't meet in a timely manner were referred to the appropriate alternate resources. In that role, I frequently attended meetings of the Warren County Ministerial Association.

Frankly, many of the Protestant ministers were a pain-in-the-ass. Their narcissistic piety, ignorance of the lived realities of poverty, and self-righteous conservatism had flattened their socio-political learning curves to level. When we needed to be discussing the nuts and bolts of delivering services effectively and efficiently, they preferred to exchange anecdotes about people they had miraculously brought to Jesus. They showed little awareness of and no respect for the constitutional limits of my role as a government employee.

[On a personal level, it didn't seem to occur to them that I might not be a Christian.]

At one of my first few meetings, there was an enthusiastic discussion about making church attendance a mandatory condition for access to the food bank and/or temporary housing.

I said, "Of course, you have the right to do that if you wish, but if you do, there will be no need for me to attend any future meetings because you will receive no referrals from DPW." This was not well received.

A Catholic priest, Father Tom Smith, came to my defense saying; "I don't think we can bring people closer to God with any combination of bribery and blackmail." He brought the discussion back around to the task at hand and got both the constitution and me off the hook. Father Smith and I became allies. The voice he brought to the meetings was a perfect-pitch blend of pragmatism and compassion. His firm, but gentle finesse in bringing errant discussions back to the job of feeding the hungry and sheltering the homeless was invaluable. Without such an ally, I doubt that I could have singlehandedly wielded sufficient authority to keep those meetings from devolving into a total waste of time, and their programs into token efforts.

When I moved on to a new job, program, and agency (within DPW), I said goodbye to the frontlines with a great sigh of relief and not a trace of nostalgia. I didn't look back. But on a more personal level, Father Smith had given objective substance to earlier, more personal impressions that inclined me to respect Catholicism more fully than any other segment of Christianity.

Though we only got together in person every two or three years, my friendship with Father Z continued. The visible goodness of his heart gave me hope in humanity itself and rendered my father-in-law's piety and devotion credible.

Years passed, and so did John and Father Z.

And then, the state Supreme Court released a grand jury report resulting from an eighteen-month investigation by the Pennsylvania Attorney General's office. I was already well aware of the shit storm in Boston (etcetera), but this was a whole state, not just a single city and it was the state where I was born and spent most of my life. When I opened the report online and scrolled down to the Erie Diocese, there were two offending priests who had served in Warren and one of them was Tom Smith. Looking into the specifics, I hoped for something that might diminish the sheer rottenness of it, but in 1987, he admitted to raping at least fifteen children, some of them as young as seven.

[Bear in mind that the Catholic Church doesn't have a monopoly on pedophilia or complicity in it's concealment—what it does have is a well-defined organizational structure and meticulous record keeping, which made it possible to track and document the abuse it was supposed to prevent.]

In reading the grand jury report, the feeling and the word that bubbles up out of the interstices between stories of abuse, the charts showing each priest's history of reassignments, the cover-ups, and the largely unspoken, but more than obvious implications of direct and indirect complicity is "evil." But throwing that word around tends to cast such a wide net that it becomes merely another four-letter word useful for its sharp, pejorative edge, but lacking the solidity of truth without considerable support. Simplistic thinking only leads either to cynical defeatism or vengeful fantasies involving flaming corncobs, scalpels, and firearms. We need to do better than that—I need to do better than that. A cathartic release of histrionic recitations of manly hypothetical violence only dissipates outrage and dishonors the morality that empowers it. Let's just drop that shit and look for clarity where it's most needed—in the heart of the confusion. This ugliness lives very close to the source of human darkness. It is light, not rage that is called for.

[One point of clarity that shouldn't be overlooked is that pedophilia is a disease. But so is psychopathy, and the active desire to harm another human being, outside of dire defense of self or loved ones, is difficult to describe as anything but sick in some fundamental way. Mental illness is a very partial exoneration.]

Lacking even the excuse of mental illness, the complicity and cover up are more reprehensible than the hidden crimes. The guilty priests acted upon aberrant urges, while their colleagues and superiors entered into a very conscious pact with their devil.

My father-in-law once told me of a humorous, old Irish prayer: "May God turn the hearts of our enemies, and if their hearts will not be turned, may he turn their ankles that we may know them by their limping."

Beneath the obvious primal outrage of children being grievously harmed by those trusted to protect them, there lurks a deep fear that our enemies walk just like we do, that evil is all around us; not only disguised with banality, but even hidden beneath layers of goodness. We fear the raw anarchy of a world in which otherwise good people do evil things, in which our enemies don't limp; they stroll blithely among us. Such a worldview renders all trust provisional and all faith pathetically naïve. It damages the spirit in a way that is a horrible reflection of the damage done to those children.

[As the adult incarnation of a battered child, with a thirty-year career in social services, I don't find the coexistence of good and evil within a single person surprising.]

A crime that compromises our ability to live in this world with the courage and good cheer requisite to redemption is treason against humanity itself. It violates a faith deeper and more fundamental than religion. It is more ugly than mere evil.

I want, I practically ache, to end this essay with at least a redeeming insight, if not something more positive. That might be easier to do if all this was as surprising as we wish it were, but countless variations on this kind of abuse have been around for a very long time and will continue to ravage the vulnerable as long as there are human beings who have power over others and are granted the presumption that their power is ordained by God or some other form of innate superiority.

The Church failed so horribly that it may well have forfeited its right to exist in its present form. But what we see via the Church's meticulous record keeping is merely the visible fifth of the proverbial iceberg. This is a failure of culture, the primal rot at the core of patriarchy.

The lesson here is that a claim to be anointed by God to wield authority over others is as sick and innately corrupt as a pedophiliac's twisted desires.

True North

I planned to follow a route that would keep me within an hour's brisk walk of the car, in case the heavy snow that was falling continued long enough to make getting back out to the main road a problem. But when the snowfall began to ebb and patches of blue appeared on the western horizon, a wordless mixture of instinct and impulse gave permission to wander.

As I let go of conscious decisions about my route of travel, I felt an ancient ease and clarity awakening in my blood. At times, I sensed the unseen nearness of animals and the mysterious reality of small omens.

A forest clearing beckoned with a strange, radiant presence. When I stepped into it, a pair of ravens flew in and circled overhead, calling out. For a moment my thoughts and their calls became entwined in a way that felt reciprocal and mutually conscious. I found myself pouring my worries, my longings, and the poignancy of my loves into their voices, wings, and wisdom in a manner best described as prayer.

I don't subscribe to a literal interpretation. If you're lost and you have a compass, it doesn't matter whether it's magnetism, God, or voodoo that directs the compass needle northward. Whether the ravens and I were actually communicating wasn't important. What mattered was where an as-if-literal response to the experience would lead me. I knew in my heart that it pointed toward the right way to live, as long as I embraced belief lightly, without attachment or righteousness. Cultivating my ability to accept the world's great mysteriousness, beyond the semantic dualisms of fact and superstition, seemed to point the way home, like a compass needle pointing north.

Orville's Antlers

I had mixed feelings about interviewing Orville in his home because he was crazy as a loon. The home visit would not be pleasant—people who smelled like Orville (a fine blend of fuel oil, wood smoke, wet dog, and stale sweat) do not tend to be good housekeepers.

But I wanted to refer Orville to the Disability Advocacy Program (DAP), and that meant I needed to get and hold his attention for at least fifteen minutes beyond the usual business of reviewing his eligibility for welfare, food stamps, and Medicaid. With someone like Orville, any strategy was a crapshoot. Coming to the office and successfully bringing all the required documents would be exponentially more difficult for him than for the more typical semi-anonymous hard-luck cases whose paperwork flowed across my desk. Though the relatively neutral environment of an interview booth in the welfare office could provide a combination of structure and intimidation that would summon more focused attention and keep the interview on track, that didn't necessarily translate into retention of what he would be told. Also, if he failed to show for the office appointment, I had to send a letter informing him that his benefits would be discontinued in ten days if he didn't contact me and comply. I didn't mind doing that with folks who were at least minimally capable, but I didn't like doing it to people whose lives had already been irremediably ravaged by various combinations of bad luck, genetics, family dysfunction, alcohol, and illness (etcetera).

The DAP referral would officially raise the issue of potential eligibility for Social Security Disability and/or and Supplemental Security Income (SSI), thus making Orville's cooperation a mandatory requirement for continued benefits from the Department of Public Welfare. When I made one of these referrals, it was imperative that I persuade the client to buy into a process they might not fully understand and could involve years of appeals. Generally, that was best accomplished through a conversation, rather than a set of recited instructions. The transition from business to conversation tended to be both smoother and more engaged in the client's home.

No one answered when I knocked on the door to the trailer that had most definitely seen better days. I walked around to the back and saw another of my clients working on a car next door.

"Have you seen Orville?"

"Yeah, he was around here a little while ago. Should be easy to spot—he's wearing purple overalls and deer antlers."

"If you see him again, tell him I was looking for him."

I drove back to the office and sent a new notice with an appointment time for an office interview and a discontinuance date, if Orville failed to show. I was responsible for well over 300 households, and my patience had to be strictly limited.

He came in at the appointed time, had all the required documents, and listened attentively to my explanation of DAP and his possible eligibility for Social Security and/or SSI benefits.

He cooperated well with his disability advocate, but the Social Security Administration rejected his application on the grounds that he was capable of working. He lost the first-level appeal, but nearly two years later, an Administrative Law Judge reversed the first two decisions and awarded Orville benefits retroactive to the original application. Orville had to reimburse the Commonwealth of Pennsylvania for welfare money he received during the appeal process, but that was less than half the sum. The lump sum benefit also made him ineligible for food stamps until the excess money dwindled to below the maximum allowable resource for a single person on food stamps. That didn't take long because he was behind on all his utility bills and in arrears to his landlord.

Orville's monthly income remained a pittance, but it was more than twice the previous pittance, and his case only had to be reviewed annually rather than every six months. By the time the next review came around, caseloads had changed. I never saw Orville again and that was okay. I wished him well, but he wasn't interesting, just nuts and sad.

A Dark Footnote

My wife's brother's son was found dead on the street in Jamestown, New York. He was thirty-one years old. I had three separate sets of memories of him. The first was of a bright, intense, fearless seven-year old. I enjoyed spending time with him and tried to give him small adventures: trout fishing, creek swimming, campfires, and hikes.

[I hoped to nourish his brightness in small ways and perhaps sow seeds of realization that might germinate in some future time of need.]

Then there was the defiant teenager who stayed with us for a summer week, surreptitiously smoked cigarettes, and biffed the unextinguished butts under our front porch. I confronted him and said, "I'm not your father and I'm not going to forbid you to smoke, but please don't play silly-assed games about it and PLEASE don't burn our house down." He continued to smoke secretively and continued to biff the butts under our porch, even after a second confrontation. I said nothing about his perfunctorily hidden stash of pornography.

[Since I thought it likely that he was more in need of openness and acceptance than authority from adult males, I tried to offer that, but he wouldn't take "yes" for an answer.]

Then, more than a decade later, there was the drug- and jail-hardened predator with cold, reptilian eyes, who made his living mostly as an enforcer for drug dealers, collecting bad debts and putting his commissions in his veins.

His grandparents (my parents-in-law) loved him with the natural, unconditional love of grandparents. He used them shamelessly, and they knew it.

Over the years, their love was toughened by practical and emotional necessity, but it never faltered.

[I worried that he would bring violent ugliness into their lives, if not directly, then through other denizens of his troubled world.]

Once when he showed up at his grandparents' home behaving strangely, I was asked to intervene and I armed myself before stepping into the situation. My presence was sufficient to defuse whatever dark scenario had been brewing.

[There was no stepping back into affection from what I had prepared myself to do.]

And then he was dead on a dark street. His grandparents wept. His father wept. My wife wept. I sighed deeply, took a long walk in the woods, and served as a pallbearer. We had all known his fate would be something like this. Justin wandered down a path that few ever have the strength to turn around and wander back home on.

[It was very poignant, but I had already mourned long ago.]

He was a junkie and all the things that junkies become: liar, thief, pimp, goon, etcetera, ad nauseum. The bright, fearless child I had cared for had been murdered by a cascade of wrong choices that just went on and on, until something both in and behind his eyes went dark, and the darkness swallowed him.

[The simple sad fact was that his passing did not make the world poorer or lesser, did not leave a hole in our lives to be slowly filled with other feelings, with other love. His death was just one more burden dumped on good, caring people who didn't deserve it.]

I meditated in the woods and fervently hoped he would do better the next time around, but I also thought it would be fine if we never met again, not even in a fresh incarnation.

1969

The trip began with a friend, who was something of a novice in the world of psychedelics and had sought my guidance. I left him in a construction site where he was trying to figure out how he had gotten to the moon. He seemed to like it there.

[We had both taken doses of LSD sufficient for two people.]

I wandered off into the night alone.

Floods of impressions, immense, overwhelming torrents of sensation were cascading over me.

[It was Saturday night during Clarion, Pennsylvania's annual Autumn Leaf Festival. The streets downtown were lined with food and craft vendors and thronged with people, and there was a carnival in the park.]

I walked quickly, while trying to maintain a calm demeanor as I headed down Main Street, away from the sensory overload of the downtown scene and toward the university campus. The sidewalk was undulating in rhythmic waves.

[I felt conspicuous, and that was probably not entirely an illusion.]

As I drew nearer to the old Catholic church, its weathered brick surface was flickering, writhing, and changing. The building metamorphosed into a huge, coiled rattlesnake, although it also remained a building in some partial way beyond explanation. Having gotten away from the hubbub of downtown, I felt calmer and began looking at the effects of the drug with a degree of dispassionate amusement. "This is one very damned interesting hallucination, even if the symbolism is a bit heavy-handed," I thought. I walked up to the building and put my hands on it, assuming there would be an interesting conflict between the visual hallucination and the tactile sensation of cool, rough brick. But it felt like snakeskin gently rising and falling with the reptile's breathing. A shiver of anxiety sent me scurrying away.

[Finding a safe haven until I reached the peak and began sliding down the far side of this trip seemed prudent.]

Sensations were no longer pouring over me in waves, but rather erupting in sharp, electric bursts too sudden and supersaturated for comprehension to grasp.

I found myself sitting on the couch at a friend's apartment without knowing how I had gotten there. But I was confident that I really was there. I was dead. I watched my body rapidly decay. Ragged hunks of putrefying flesh fell from my bones. I was a skeleton. My bones began to crumble.

With a sudden, electric jolt, I was inexplicably whole and living again.

A very pretty young woman was looking into my eyes.

"Do want some tea, Reg?"

"Yes, that would be great. Thanks."

On the stereo Jim Morrison sang softly, "I am the lizard king...."

We were making love on the living room floor when another woman with whom I sometimes shared tender but uncommitted eros walked in and then fled in great haste.

[I hadn't seen myself as sufficiently lovable to cause the sadness that streamed out behind her like some strange vapor as she rushed out of the room, down the stairs, and into the street.]

We awoke in the morning, entwined on the living room floor. The large candle that had burned beside us illuminating our bodies with flickering light had melted into a hardened pool on the carpet. I rolled a couple of joints while she cooked oatmeal.

Bartleby's Choice

I was around seven when I first found myself so hopelessly tangled in one of my parents' chronic, crazy, and irresolvable double binds that I felt consciously suicidal. I spoke up about how I felt. I spoke frantically because I *was* frantic. The situation seemed seriously dire—I was afraid I might really do it, even though I preferred not to. They responded by beating the shit out of me for saying something so terrible, so obviously and selfishly intended to hurt *them*.

[Though I couldn't articulate it, I recognized the dark abyss of their narcissism.]

I survived because I had books, woods to hide out in, a trusted brother, and Pete, a parentally exiled dog I visited secretly. I learned to keep my mouth shut and cultivated silent stoicism in the bottom layers of depression.

[Frankly, my emotional state was such that being stuck in it without hope of reprieve might very well have constituted valid grounds to cancel my ticket and bail out.]

Glimpsing that ultimate option up close and possible changed me in a lasting way. I have lived each day since as a conscious choice, because I gave myself full permission to pull the plug a very long time ago. In truth, I usually make a committed choice every two to five years. When I try to project much beyond that, the future quickly blurs into abstraction as possibilities multiply and become more random. That's how it works for me, how I survive. Frankly, I find it less scary than the default setting for most people, which is to simply blunder forward until one day they fall. I find that seriously, fucking crazy. I need a tighter grasp than that.

[Life is voluntary. It's not a default setting; it's a choice. Consciousness makes it so.]

The few people I've told about this have found it very sad and at least a little bit crazy, but I don't think of it that way. Though it obviously came from a time of great sadness, it is a rational method that has kept me alive into my eighth decade, and as I blunder on into my geezer years, I have so much work to finish (writing and painting) and love to cherish that running out of time has become a much bigger concern than checking out early.

[My method is not something I can, in good conscience, recommend to others because it involves an open embrace of suicide as an option, and I came close a couple of times. Calling your own bluffs can be a serious gamble. But if you've already been dealt that hand, fuck faith and trust your art.]

I am here because I would prefer not to leave.

Fire, Feces, and Healthcare

My grandfather was born in 1900, in a small village in Forest County, Pennsylvania. During his early teens, his neighborhood was inhabited by a fairly standard curmudgeon—a perennially ornery character who confiscated baseballs that landed in his yard, and shouted angrily at children who took a shortcut across his covetously owned property. Naturally, the neighborhood kids hated him.

One Halloween, my grandfather and his friends decided to go well beyond the realm of soaped windows and smashed pumpkins in their annual rite of revenge against the tormented soul who tormented them. They picked up the man's outhouse, moved it back several feet, and laid sticks and leaves over the pit to disguise their trap. Shortly before sunrise the following morning, their victim made his customary trip to the privy and fell into the hole.

Unable to extricate himself, the man yelled, as loudly as he could, "Fire! Fire!" All the adults in the neighborhood came running to the scene immediately, bearing buckets, shovels, and axes. After they rescued him from his predicament, someone asked, "Why did you yell 'fire'?" He replied, "Would you have come running to help if I'd yelled 'shit'?"

The desperate man yelled "fire" because a house fire was a huge catastrophe that could strike by such sheer happenstance or small oversight that it was universally perceived as an affliction of innocents. Coping with it was regarded as a collective responsibility. Such shared responsibility has, for millennia, been one of the founding principles not only of community, but of civilization itself.

In a small village, all it took for the shared responsibility of dealing with a fire's horrific threat to be recognized and summoned was a shout or perhaps, a bell. As communities grew to encompass distances beyond earshot, and rising individual anonymity veiled personal disasters in abstraction, coping with collective responsibilities became more organized. A small town needs a volunteer fire department. A city needs a crew of full-time professionals. Instead of running to the scene with a bucket, we now respond to a scream of "fire" with a phone call to 911 and an annual tax bill. *No one calls this socialism.*

There is no movement to abolish fire departments and replace them with corporate, profit-making enterprises (which would bill the victims of disaster for their services) on the grounds that such enterprises would be intrinsically more efficient and effective. Although I'm sure they carry their standard, inevitable share of human dysfunction, I've encountered no credible suggestion that fire departments are doomed to inadequacy and fiscal irresponsibility by virtue of being governmental agencies. I believe the same could be said of our police and military forces. But the reason any proposal to privatize these aspects of government would be generally regarded as absurd is at least as universal as theoretical cynicisms about the mythical impossibility of governmental efficiency. The needs they address are fundamental aspects of the collective responsibility that is the raison d'être of community and government. As such, they do not rationally or morally belong in the realm of commerce. The values they represent are not, and should not be, for sale.

Consider the fundamental purpose of government. It's not something defined by a constitution. The purpose of a constitution is to confine the action and power of government within a structure, so that it can effectively fulfill its purpose without violating individual rights in overzealous or misguided pursuit of that purpose. The purpose of government is to act as the agent of society's collective responsibility. I realize I've taken something worthy of a long book and reduced it to a couple of sentences here, but the mostly ignored issues at hand in the current pseudo-debates about healthcare are so fundamental that there is far more risk of simplistic thinking to be found in arguments about pre-existing conditions or public options than in bringing the discussion down to the level of basic moral, social, and philosophical issues.

Though the ways and means may differ, human freedom is as constrained in an authoritarian society with a democratic government as it is in an open, democratic society with an authoritarian government. Protecting the open space of democracy is a collective responsibility that extends far beyond simplistic definitions of legal rights. This is why we have public schools and public libraries. Without universal access to education for the young, and to all forms of literary culture for adults, society would devolve into feudalism with frightening rapidity—a calamity every bit as devastating as an earthquake or flood. We do not abandon these things to the limited and capricious mercies of the marketplace because nurturing the spirit of democracy is a responsibility and a blessing shared by all; they are not items of commerce. Everyone benefits from living in an educated, literate, well-informed society.

In a civilized society, the sick, wounded, and infirm are neither shot nor eaten. They are not abandoned. We pay taxes to support schools, police, fire departments, the military, libraries, and a postal system. When someone runs from a house screaming "fire", we call 911 and perhaps run to help. But what is the greater undeserved calamity, a house fire (assuming the occupants escape relatively unscathed) or pancreatic cancer? In this country, when someone cries out "cancer!" or "heart attack!" or when someone who makes minimum wage and drives twenty-five miles each way to work cries out "My child has a sinus infection and the antibiotic of choice costs $150!", any claim to collective responsibility is dismissed as "socialism".

If we lack the common decency to be ashamed of our lack of compassion, we ought to at least be angered by the insult to our intelligence; the straw man of socialism is bullshit so shallow it would embarrass any self-respecting con man. Indeed, it is the degradation of health-care to a market-driven commercial enterprise that is functionally an instrument of repression.

By taking the place of government in addressing a basic aspect of natural collective responsibility, the health insurance industry is a de facto government controlling our health care from outside the constitutional and moral constraints of democratic government and social responsibility. The health insurance industry's profits are *taxes* paid into the pockets of its leaders (and their corporate shareholders) rather than their ostensible purpose of protecting us from calamities that are often far worse than fire or flood. Taxes levied and taken by authorities other than a legitimate, democratic government are taxation without representation and should be regarded just as the founding fathers regarded such taxation—as tyranny and thievery.

Requiring a family to mortgage their home in order to keep their child alive is not entrepreneurship or even capitalism; it is extortion. That it is legal in this country does not diminish the intrinsic criminality of its spirit any more than it excused the Nazis who engineered the Holocaust or the soldiers who eviscerated unarmed Native American women and children. To call it free enterprise is a vicious insult to every independent businessperson, entrepreneur, farmer, and crafts person in America. Hell, it should insult drug dealers, mobsters, and prostitutes, who all stand on moral high ground by comparison.

Is universal health-care a right? Perhaps that doesn't even matter. Providing universal health care is a responsibility we all share by virtue of being civilized. Our failure to embrace it as a collective responsibility has nothing to do with free markets, socialism, the Bill of Rights, the theories of Karl Marx, or even concerns about administrative efficiency; it is savagery.

Our political leaders have not, and are unlikely to truly address this issue, and it's not because they've chosen to take a tough, principled stand as guardians of our liberty—it's because they don't want to. They're afraid that attempting to row against the torrent of right-wing swill pouring forth from the health insurance industry and talk radio into the public's collective cynicism and fear would dump political careers in the outhouse. Without the votes of Bubba and Bubbette, our elected representatives might lose their jobs and their health insurance.

The pervasive, institutionalized anxiety of an insurance-dependent system contributes to a widespread spirit of apathy, impotence, and defeatism that is toxic to all the social and political possibilities of democracy. You're not going to see much dissent or even thinking outside the box coming from people whose families will lose access to healthcare if they lose their job. You're not going to see people up to their necks (or over their heads) in medical debt seeking creative new career possibilities. People living in constant, solitary fear— whether of fire, lawlessness, foreign aggression, or medical catastrophe—cannot be truly free in mind and spirit, regardless of the legal rights guaranteed to them by a constitution. Our insurance-dependent system is the whip that drives the galley slaves rowing the ship of state. A single-payer public healthcare system would not diminish democracy; it would enable and enhance it and, frankly, that's why both sides of the aisle are yelling "shit" instead of "fire".

I would like to believe that the semi-literate demagogues who are braying so loudly that universal healthcare would be the beginning of the end of American freedom are merely deluded, but I suspect the reality is far sleazier than mere dysfunction. There's nothing we can say to them that wouldn't apply equally to the horses they rode in on.

Manufactured Darkness

We Americans like to think of our national character as having been shaped by the rugged individualism of pioneers bringing civilization to savage wilderness. This is largely a lie. The wilderness gave us a sense of primal freedom that we have breathed through like a straw to keep from drowning in drudgery, fear, and futility, but the true shaping force that has defined our character is the constant trauma of war.

[America has been at war for more than ninety percent of its history.]

Over the past two decades, America has settled into docile acceptance of perpetual war as a matter-of-fact condition of modern life. Our young soldiers come home in flag-draped coffins, while political hacks and hustlers deflect our rage and grief with simplistic blather about patriotism, glory, and noble sacrifice. The mass media lap it up and spew it forth, while we re-elect the real killers and fetishize our guns. We are an individually, collectively, politically, and economically violent nation.

[When I was a welfare caseworker I once filed a report that resulted in a child being removed from his parents' household. In protective custody, he wept inconsolably because he missed his daddy, who had tied him to a chair and burned him with cigarettes.]

American gun fetishism is largely the result of the inability of most men to conjure a vision of manliness not defined by fantasies of histrionic violence. The gunners present their fear of losing their guns as a brave, noble, and manly defense of freedom, which (of course) can only be protected by loud threats of violence. But the loss they truly fear is of their manliness and its glorious empowerment by rage.

[We have to deal with this—it is eating us alive.]

Only culture can repair the damaged hearts and spirits of our males. We need to have a multi-layered public discourse, not merely about guns, but about the tectonics of the many layers of war trauma that have shaped our collective and individual psychic landscape. We have to lay bare our ravaged hearts with a new kind of ruthless courage.

[The stories my father told about his youth were mostly macho tales of muscular feats, fierce fists, and hot tempers. I realized long before I could articulate it, that if you peeled away the language that defined the shiny surface of his boasting, all was raw pathos.]

As the adult incarnation of a battered child, I can see the aching roots of violence at work in my own psyche. The right blend of chemistry and carefully navigated mood can push the darkness in my heart over the horizon for a while, but eventually the balance slips, and the shadow returns.

[The violent-male-as-hero paradigm has been chanted in the background noise of culture since we blundered out of the Pleistocene, but since the beginnings of cinema, violence has been glamorized, polished to a shine, and sugarcoated. Casually ravenous for the sweetness of "wow," we've eagerly lapped up the torrential swill of synthetic spectacle. Glamorized violence has become programmed into our sense of worldly possibility in a way that is utterly disproportionate to its statistical or anecdotal reality. It is bullshit. We need to stop eating it. This is one aspect of the problem of social violence that lives outside the realm of government. This is cultural. We, the people, own it.]

I believe in nonviolence. I arrived at that belief in the confluence of Buddhism, the peace and civil rights movements, and the zeitgeist of the late 1960s. I am a capable skeptic, and my belief in nonviolence has weathered decades of relentless critical thought. Still, I've never succeeded in fully internalizing it. My capacity for violence was given to me in a way that cannot be given back.

[My childhood was steeped in brutal dysfunction, but to define me or the violence in my heart in terms of that alone is pathetically simplistic.]

I'm capable of some really fucking awful shit.

[Is that simply the zeitgeist?]

If I am faced with an aggressive drunk or a direct physical threat to myself, a defenseless innocent, or someone I love, things can get extremely ugly at light speed, and I'm pretty good at taking the lead in the ugliness. I've managed to stay out of serious trouble by cultivating my ability to see these things coming and steer in another direction. But sometimes, there is neither enough space nor enough time to maneuver.

[When a deer knocked senseless by a head-on collision with my truck enveloped me in a flurry of hooves, one of which struck my face, I drew my knife and killed him before I had consciously processed what was happening.]

Beyond our various evolving opinions about gun laws, social programs, healthcare, and the Constitution, we have a collective problem that lives independently in each of us. We have to change. The changes we need to bring to our culture begin in our individual hearts and minds.

[Yes, I realize how sappy that sounds.]

Returning the adult incarnation of a battered child to the emotional condition of his battering is risky business. Though Mr. Hyde has saved Dr. Darling's ass a few times, he has more often been a source of danger, difficulty, and embarrassment. I am unable to feel the macho pride so many other males seem to find in the confluence of urgency and dysfunction. I don't like the person I can become when the need arises—even when the need is real and just.

[Outside the realm of heavy adrenaline provocation, gentleness remains my default setting.]

This dissonance complicates my advocacy of the peacefulness I truly believe is humankind's only hope.

[Though I've never tended to see myself as typifying much of anything, the dissonance in my heart feels larger than me—it feels collective.]

Our darkness isn't wild; it is civilized.

Down on the Farm

I met Larry in the circle of artists, intellectuals (sort of), and misfits who gathered regularly at the Plaza Restaurant in downtown Warren, Pennsylvania to get buzzed on caffeine and carry on long rambling conversations about politics, art, music, books, philosophy, and life in Warren. Larry was a nattily dressed, fifty-ish, one-legged minister who seemed a bit out of place in our motley crew, but he had a lively sense of humor and an open-mindedness I had rarely seen in people heavily occupied with evangelical Christianity.

[Larry lost his right leg in a car accident when he was a teenager and the amputation was too far above the knee to allow use of a functional prosthesis. He walked using a pair of forearm crutches.]

That Larry's sense of humor extended to both his religion and his disability earned considerable redemption for the ways he would otherwise have been an oxymoron in our midst. His self-deprecating wit was actually endearing in its insincerity—he tried to be humble, but it wasn't easy.

[We were all at least a little ostentatious in our displays of post-hippie cynicism, and there was more testosterone involved in our noble (tragically hip) posturing than any of us would have admitted.]

He seemed untroubled by our countless variations on a theme of irreverence.

March 6, 1986: At the office yesterday, the rate of interruption was so high and constant that the typically half-hour job of writing up a food stamp recertification took from 11:00 AM until 4:00 PM. I stayed an extra hour and a half at the end of the day trying to get caught up, but my progress was negligible.

[I was a caseworker with the Warren County office of the Pennsylvania Department of Public Welfare.]

In the evening, I tried in vain to paint, but couldn't muster the requisite concentration. I played with Oren [my three-year old son] for a while and fell asleep on the couch.

At times, I'm not sure whether my art is inspiration or dysfunction. But when I think about giving up, I wonder if I could fill the huge space that would leave in my life with anything but petty, stupid hedonism.

It sounds fine and noble to talk about heroically or obsessively sustaining passion solely with your own inner resources, but in truth you'll eventually bleed yourself dry. There's a good chance that an instinct for self-preservation will kick in before you reach the empty bottom, but the result isn't likely to be pretty or happy.

Larry was the apparent leader of a group of people who lived communally on a small farm tucked away on a dirt road in the Allegheny National Forest. The four women, Dee-Dee, Kim, Laura, and Pam, were soft-spoken, visibly intelligent, and accomplished musicians. They came to town each weekday and fanned out to the various housecleaning jobs that provided the farm with much of its cash flow.

The only other male, besides Larry, was Rob, a young man (mid-twenties, probably) who slept outside nearly all year. He seemed bright and cheerful, but didn't say much.

[I had a persistent intuition that Rob was living hidden for reasons other than the state of his soul.]

March 21, 1986: Getting to know the people at Windy Ridge Farm better and liking them a lot—good people who live close to the Earth. They're Christians who don't try to ram their faith down one's throat, as so many others do.

March 26, 1986: Ego delighting in virtuosity as insights erupt from the singing of colors. It's no coincidence that my confidence surges with the coming of spring. Though I do better at dodging the winter doldrums as I age, winter still comes upon my spirit just as it blankets the land. The seasons are a metaphorical cycle of birth, growth, death, and rebirth we carry within us and see mirrored in nature—hope arising from cold and darkness like the lotus sprouting from muck.

It wasn't long before I was invited to visit Larry's farm and brought my wife, Terry and our children, Holly, and Oren. We felt matter-of-factly welcome and at ease there.

Windy Ridge Farm became a comfortable place of music, conversation, and animals (horses, goats, rabbits, chickens, sheep, pigs, and cattle) that stood outside the busyness and stress of our lives. The animals were a delight to both Holly and Oren, and the close-to-the-land lifestyle seemed a healthy counterpoint to the influences of the dominant (television) culture.

The house was Spartan, but comfortable. One first-floor room, the parlor, was occupied by rows of wooden chairs. The large blackboard was often filled with complex diagrams and biblical names, but Christian beliefs were never aggressively or inappropriately forced into conversation.

Oren said, "Ducks aren't like us. They have funny feet and they don't have knees like we do."

May 5, 1986: The first thing I must face in this Monday morning office is a mistake I made that probably caused a family some serious hardship—apologize and fix it—there's no time for guilt. I've been doing this job too long to be too hugely sensitive about such things, but it's a hell of way to start a week.

May 7, 1986: Larry is trying, in a gentle way, to convert me. Yesterday, he spoke about specifically Christian spiritual experiences. I fully realize the sense of reality, validity, and objective truth such experiences give to the body of belief that forms their context, but I've had my own such experiences, and they were very specifically Buddhist. That's where all philosophical argument ends with regard to differences of religion. Whose experience is more "real," yours or mine? From my standpoint, that's not even a valid question—both are real and valid in terms of our respective karmic situations. It's difficult for Christians to have that kind of openness—for them the situation is vastly more urgent because they see this life as a one and only chance at a salvation to be eternally won or irrevocably lost.

May 16, 1986: I took Oren fishing last evening, but (as I was as a child) he was more interested in following his wandering attention through the forest than in something as purposeful and focused as fishing. Right now his attention is drawn to flowers, so I'll go with that. We'll look at flowers, identify them, learn about them, etcetera. Flowers are a fine vehicle for wandering.

When I met Jude for lunch today, he showed me copies of some old newspaper articles about the demise of Larry's religious community near Ashtabula. The stories seem clumsily exaggerated, but also not without substance—indoctrination, militarism, and severe discipline, including beatings serious enough to bring the authorities down on them for child abuse. A long past episode of religious hysteria? I'm glad Jude brought it to my attention. These folks seem open and gentle, but a bit of wariness is in order here.

Terry and I agreed that we should grant the folks at the farm the assumption that the alleged events in their old community in Ohio were part of some sort of past craziness these eminently down-to-Earth people had since grown far beyond. Larry was a fifty-fifty mix of bullshit and brilliance, but Windy Ridge Farm was a place of fertility and self-sufficiency. Though we made a mutual, conscious decision to give these folks a chance, we also agreed that common sense called for vigilance.

It wasn't a bad choice for us. Holly and Oren got to interact with the animals and received kind, gentle attention from the women. The pleasures were simple and direct. The food was wholesome, and Larry had expensive scotch tucked away in a kitchen cupboard. Art and music were cherished and respected. The way everyone worked together looked a lot like love.

June 25, 1986: In the painting I finished last night there is a point near the right edge where the placement of almost anything would have created a basic, satisfying, visually comfortable equilibrium. The decision not to put something there was a small denial of compositional skill, a refusal to be facile that took more courage than a non-artist would be likely to understand.

June 30, 1986: Loving Terry—the feeling rises and subsides like ocean waves. Too often, the conscious mind loses track of love amidst the bustle and busyness of all that must be done. Unconscious channels of communication get clogged with debris. Cues get misunderstood and insecurities arise. The ways of being fully (or at least adequately) attentive to love have to be continually reinvented lest one mistake an obsolete method for a dying out of love itself.

On the other hand, the women deferred to Larry with a completeness that courted self-satire. Their clothing was plain and nineteenth-century utilitarian. His scarves were silk and his coat mohair. The constantly changing, dense diagrams on the wall-spanning chalkboard in the first floor "parlor" clearly indicated that Larry conducted intensive teaching sessions grounded in many layers of scriptural esoterica.

July 21, 1986: Sunday morning breakfast at Windy Ridge Farm—a movie for the kids and a horseback riding lesson—the first time I've been on a horse since I was a child. I was amazed at the easy responsiveness of the horse to my directions. I'm tempted to learn more, but it seems like an extraordinarily high maintenance avocation.

After he spent a day with my parents, I asked Oren, "Did you have a good time?"

"Yeah, we went fishing."

"Did you catch anything?"

"Papa caught a big trout. We put him in a bucket and took him home and he was our friend. Then we ate him."

Larry and I had long, rambling conversations that sometimes ventured forthrightly into religion and spirituality. We educated each other about our differing perspectives and that summoned both eloquence and precision. It was challenging in a way that was mostly positive. Larry had difficulty understanding Buddhism because he was very addicted to his dualities—couldn't imagine life or thought without them. But (at first) he didn't proselytize; there was a genuine dialogue.

I had left my family's Christianity behind long ago. Though my new faith had been variously disputed, disparaged, dismissed, and condemned, I was never challenged philosophically or even poetically. My parental family was a brick wall in that respect. There was no possibility of dialogue.

Standing up to and engaging Larry's really quite gentle and respectful conversion pitches—directly rejecting them as gently and respectfully as they had been offered was therapeutic. It helped me put away some unfinished business, but defending my faith would have eventually become terminally tedious if it had gone on too long.

November 3, 1986: When Oren's grandmother gave him a Halloween flashlight, he immediately began talking about going into the caves at Rimrock. On Sunday, when I took him there, he surprised me with how far into a cave he was willing to go before wanting to turn back. After the cave we walked on to the far end of the overlook area where Oren wanted to sit on a rock and talk for a while, which we did for about twenty minutes. A short distance farther on, he came upon a rock that reminded him of a boat, so he sat on it and paddled with a stick for a few minutes.

Back home, Terry had errands to run, so I cooked dinner—and broke off a large portion of a tooth on the first bite. After the kids went to bed, Terry and I watched a movie and made love on the living room floor.

Oren watched very intently while I skinned a deer. He was silent for a long time and then said, "Deers can fly."

"Really?"

"Yeah, they just have to pretend they have wings and they can fly like a dragon."

"That would make them really tough to hunt."

He laughed and said, "You can't eat dragons."

"Why not?"

"They have too much fire inside them."

December 19, 1986: *Deer season is over and the freezer is filled with our winter's meat.*

During long, solitary days meditating while waiting for deer, utterly absorbed in my senses, there were periods of near mystical communion with the forest, reminding me of a need for a renewal of spiritual practice in my day-to-day life—more zazen at least and more hunter's attention to the unmediated here and now.

Walter was a transient, but he didn't turn up anywhere on Pennsylvania's welfare computer system. He was crazy. He had that trapped animal look in his eyes that told you to be ready to hit him with a chair if he moved too suddenly. He talked and talked and talked, leaving no opportunity for me to cut to the chase and find out how much rent he paid, how to verify it, and where he lived before he came to Warren County, without thwarting him in a way that could get ugly.

I needed to determine that he was residing in Pennsylvania for reasons other than a vacation. A couple of weeks earlier, I had denied food stamps to a busload of Rainbow People on their way to a gathering in the Allegheny National Forest for that very reason. I also needed to determine that any benefits he received from Pennsylvania would not overlap benefits already received in another state.

He said he thought he would be staying here a while because it looked like it would be safe. When I questioned what he meant, he said he had found something incredible, something of vast importance for the future of the whole human race. As a result of his discovery, several mysterious groups of people were out to get him.

I kept trying to segue out of his rambling, incoherent tale of vast conspiracies, hidden powers, and his unique, but unasked for, ability to forestall the coming apocalypse, into questions about where and when he last received benefits, his financial resources, and how to verify his identity. His emotional state vacillated wildly in a mixture of agitation, distrust, euphoria, furtiveness, and desperation. Some of it was play-acting and some of it wasn't. He clearly thought himself to be extraordinarily clever.

Walter kept referring again and again to the vast importance of what he had found, hinting that, if I only knew and understood, I would sweep away all those petty regulations and give him all the help he needed. Finally I asked, "Just what is it you've found?"

"I'll show you, but don't tell anyone. It could put your life in danger."

"Don't worry Walter, I'm no hero. I'm just trying to help you. I don't want to call any unwanted attention to you by filing a benefits application with any irregularities on it."

He reached into his knapsack and took out a paper bag from which he produced a nondescript gray rock the size of a lemon.

"See what I mean? It's incredible, isn't it?"

I felt a weird, mixed rush of comedy and fear. I was wearing down. I had spent forty-five minutes in an eight-foot square room with a bona fide lunatic, while my desk was piled with unprocessed applications. I really didn't want to have to explain to some unemployed single mother that her food stamps would be late or she wouldn't be able to pay her rent on time because I had spent the morning talking to a madman about his pet rock.

"I was just walking along the road and there it was. I've been on the run ever since."

"Well Walter, I think when something this important comes into your life, you need to understand it as well as possible so you know what to do next. This is no time to make the wrong move."

"Yeah, you're right; that's what worries me."

I told him he should go to the headquarters of the Allegheny National Forest in downtown Warren and ask to speak to a geologist. I assured him that they could be trusted. He thanked me profusely and rushed out of the office, eager to unlock the secrets of the universe and the fate of mankind.

Later that day, the phone rang. It was someone with the Allegheny National Forest. "Don't ever do that to me again," she said.

I issued Walter a one-month food stamp allotment, and he never returned.

January 7, 1987: *Slow start (morning).*

Slide through the world with as little impact as possible—is that the way?

Spend the rest of my life as a bureaucrat? It seems pretty likely and I'm learning to accept it, As human lives go on planet Earth, I'm extraordinarily fortunate, but knowing that statistically supported fact really doesn't help much. Acceptance requires much more than comparisons with third world horror and disease. Acceptance accrues gradually as the ego is slowly battered into submission and transformations hoped for with naïve eagerness fail to arrive.

Oren teaches me the joy and wisdom of simply being here (now). I hope he finds his way to healthy realism more quickly than I did.

Would it have been better not to have so many grand pipe dreams?

My work remains free, protected by reality from my clumsy, foolish efforts to sell it.

January 9, 1987: *A painting sketched in and taped to the board on my easel awaits me at home.*

(Friday, at last.)

Intense office action.

Donuts

Weariness

Coffee

Blood pressure 110/70

Refusing to daydream.

I am a bureaucrat. I have no "career." The proper realm for my ambition(s) is the quality of my art, not my clueless efforts to manipulate its fate. If I am to go on with my work, the working assumption has to be that my life's work will be a posthumous project. Efforts to the contrary tend to bring suffering in proportion to my attachment. Without my family and my art, there would be nothing left of me but hunting and hedonism.

Watching the clock—counting down through the last minutes of the workday.

One of my welfare clients was a hardworking guy, not unintelligent, but not particularly brilliant either.

[Many of my clients were like him in that way.]

He had always been poor, even when he was working and he lived in a barn load of bad luck with a quiet dignity that was a pretty clean rendition of what quiet dignity humbly means.

His fourteen-year old daughter got into a physical altercation with another girl at school. In the subsequent counseling session with the school's guidance counselor she attributed her errant behavior to her distress over being raped by her father.

The man's arrest made the front page of the local newspaper. The dismissal of charges made page five of section B. He became a pariah in his homeland, and then my official, non-forwarding mail was returned. I closed his case.

[I don't even remember his name.]

January 13, 1987: Fencing last evening was wonderfully intense. Whole bouts of pure Zen. I fenced very hard and aggressively out of an overabundance of energy, which made me sloppy when form and attention wavered, but yielded amazing, complex perfections whenever flowing attention briefly approached purity. Afterward I was quietly ecstatic.

Later, at home, making love with Terry, I was immersed in that same transcendent flow and carried its warm light with me into sleep. I awoke this morning with fresher energy than I've felt in too long.

January 14, 1987: In court today on a welfare fraud prosecution, I was spared testimony by a guilty plea. No matter how disgusting, foolish, drunk, dirty, and/or stupid the defendants are, I loathe testifying against them. Their lives are already more punishment than most of them deserve. I accept their prosecution as the intersection of their karma and mine, but I lack the requisite self-righteousness to find satisfaction in furthering their misfortune.

The Claim Settlement guy loves it. A prosecution is his idea of good, clean fun. Sometimes, he works on prosecutions at home for the sheer pleasure of it. He's a strange man. He carries a large, leather-bound Bible in his briefcase for coffee break and lunch hour reading. He was a conscientious objector during Vietnam. His favorite pastime is watching television wrestling. He brushes his teeth once weekly whether they need it or not, and farts loudly and often without excusing himself. A co-worker compared the sound to someone trying to start an outboard motor.

Larry asked some fairly specific and thoughtful questions about Buddhism and the ensuing discussion led seamlessly (by unrecalled means) to his concerns about his own life. He said he had been thinking he should take a wife. He thought that marriage would settle his spirit in a way that would make him a better man and a better minister. The question for him was which of the women at the farm should be his choice. I was a taken aback by his casual assumption that he could simply choose one, and the question made me uncomfortable in several ways, not the least of which was my belief in romantic love as a kind of spiritual imperative.

[I also found Pam uncomfortably attractive even though I was wholly in love and happily monogamous with Terry.]

I said, "You need hunger—the selfless greed of wanting infinitely more of another's presence. I couldn't settle for less than that, though I realize most people do. I tried it a few times and it didn't work."

[This was not a very Buddhist response.]

February 24, 1987: Beethoven's Ninth on my headphones.
Warhol is dead. His importance is greater than the sum of his works.
(Artist as critic in drag?)
In keeping with his life and work, his absence will now function with the definiteness of a presence.

Larry tried to lay a conversion pitch on me again and I hope I laid it firmly to rest. I told him that I respect the authenticity of his own conversion experience, but it's the Buddha who has spoken to me, and until I have fully answered to that, it would be dishonest and unrealistic to dick around with Christianity.

My respect for Larry is declining. Though, at times, I enjoy his conversation, his politics flirt with fascism in a way that's beneath his intelligence and far from Christian. And the way others at the farm labor to support not merely his wisdom, but his dandyism—silk scarf and mohair coat— tends to disgust me even though it's none of my business.

The first cracks in my friendship with Larry radiated out from the impacts of his increasingly undisguised conversion pitches. I handled those as I did with anyone. I used them as starting points for speculation and expression (rather than treat them as endpoints anchored in certainty) and expressed appreciation for the mutual illumination of differing viewpoints. At first, Larry went along with that, but gradually his efforts became more pointed until, eventually, I had to be blunt and tell him that I had my own faith and though I was willing to talk about almost anything, abandoning my faith was not open to discussion.

[I had expected this to happen eventually—Christians tend to be that way.]

For a while, our conversations moved back toward mutual acceptance and respect.

March 19, 1987: Larry loaned me a book that purports to be a Christian analysis of Modernism. It's a piece of pathetic trash full of simplistic thinking and outright lies. It's disappointing because the connective tissue throughout the text is stupidity—seriously, I'm not being pissed off or arrogant here. It's fucking stupid, and I can see that Larry genuinely took it to heart. I thought him brighter than that.

March 26, 1987: *I worry over the genuineness of the persistent pain and pathos, the anguish and, at times, frenzy in my images. One could credibly ask, "If this isn't pretentious exaggeration, how have you stood it?" The simple answer is, "Not very well, it's wearing me down."*

Clarifying the nature of my suffering through an expressive medium distances it enough to prevent gross interference with the things I need to do in order to function in the world and to sociably maintain a credible simulation of at least partial contentment.

(In some ways that's a haven and in some ways it's a trap.)

There seems to be a broad social trend going on—the malaise of the 80s— people living their lives through a series of credible simulations without the benefit of theater's "willing suspension of disbelief." The critical aesthetic issue seems to be the choice of whether to accept that situation.

(Perhaps we flatter ourselves with the notion that we have a choice.)

My reflexive reaction in and through my work is to resist—to try to make paintings that cannot be simulations; that can only be realities. But it's difficult to find emotional balance because the moneyed world has sucked cash from simulations of pleasure for so many centuries that nearly all our viable symbols of joy have been rendered counterfeit, leaving pain more accessible to direct, honest expression.

At times lately, I've doubted the possibility of resistance—wondered if the rebellious urge is not itself merely a credible simulation standing in for remnant idealism that is, itself, no longer credible.

Life in the 80s seems to be a crazy patchwork of veneers, and when you poke holes in them, what shows through is suffering. Self-awareness determines the degree to which the suffering is conscious, but regardless of whether its conscious or unconscious, it's there.

The facade is so full of cracks and holes that realism can no longer be both literal and true. Multicolored and multilayered reality leaks though in gushes and trickles that are mostly composed of angst, alienation, pathos, desire, and confusion rendered bearable and sometimes strangely beautiful by sex, music, art, meditation, kinesthesia, and intoxication.

So we shouldn't question the pain we paint.

I think it takes either a fool or a genius to understate it—what requires integrity is to refuse to oversimplify into platitudes, cynicism, or entertainment.

April 1, 1987: *I have to be careful not to deny myself happiness by oversimplifying my concept of it. It's not a thing you have, but rather something* *you do. I'm not good enough at it to tell anyone how to do it, but I do know that it's not a pure, unalloyed state or process. It is not bliss.*

In the café at the Albright-Knox Gallery, Oren put the pepper shaker to his nose, inhaled, then sneezed and said, "I like to sneeze."

Larry invited Terry and me to give a fencing demonstration at the farm. He said he was interested in it partly as a self-defense skill for the women—one could easily substitute a stick, broom handle, umbrella, or cane for a foil—but he was also simply curious about it as a sport pursued avidly by his friends. He said he also had a neighbor who was interested. I enjoyed teaching fencing and I came to the farm that day looking forward to an opportunity to share something from my world with these people who had generously shared so much of their world with me.

After Terry and I did our basic demo, the neighbor wanted to try. At first, he balked at donning a jacket and mask, but relented when I pointed out that, without safety equipment, he would be betting his life that my blade wouldn't break. But then it got weird.

"I bet I can put you on the ground in less than two minutes."

"This is fencing—we don't put people on the ground; we score points."

"There aren't any points in a fight."

I removed my mask, laid my foil on the ground, and said, "This isn't a fight."

"That's what I came here for."

"Then, you're talking to the wrong guy. If I wanted to hurt you, I would hide in those trees over there and shoot you in the back."

[Adrenaline was pumping hard, and my intelligence had turned three-quarters reptile.]

After a moment of tense silence, I added, "Seriously man, think of it as contact tennis. I think we're done here for today."

I began packing up my gear.

Through all of this, Larry watched intently, but said nothing. My gut feeling was that Larry wasn't wholly innocent in this man's misguided expectations. I was angry and offended, but I knew better than to be confrontational on the downhill side of an adrenaline rush.

Larry seemed quietly chagrinned—he had tried to do something and it hadn't worked. I didn't know if it was me or the twisted neighbor who derailed his imagined scenario. I tried to grant Larry the benefit of the doubt and assume that it was the neighbor who brought violent intentions to the situation, but that assumption didn't yield enough redemption to cover my feelings. A man had gotten physically threatening and aggressive with me while I was a guest at Larry's home. In my world, threatening a guest in my home with unwarranted violence got you ordered off the premises and probably dropkicked off the edge of my universe. Larry's reaction was one of mild disappointment. My disappointment was not mild.

[It's partly an old redneck male thing; when you're threatened, your (true) friends are supposed to step up and stand shoulder to shoulder with you.]

I became more alert in my interactions with Larry. I applied critical thinking that I wouldn't normally apply in social situations—not because I had any particular suspicions, but because, when I find myself unable to make intuitive or emotional sense of my situation, the old philosophy major sits up and takes notice.

June 8, 1987: Paintings I can't help believing in flow forth as performances with the total, immediate intensity of fencing, danger, orgasm—orgasmic Zen? Zen is surely there at the heart of it, but it is just as surely not tranquil. The Buddha partners with Dionysius in this process.

Later that summer, Windy Ridge Farm hosted an outdoor dinner gathering for friends and the people the women worked for in town. Pam and Kim (sisters) played music that was both heartfelt and beautifully precise. The atmosphere was welcoming and the sense of mutual welcoming between the community and the farm was heartening to see in Warren, where xenophobia was (and is) endemic and eccentricity was (and is) regarded with suspicion.

[I wondered if perhaps some of the various lessons of the sixties were finally settling into rural Amurka.]

When Larry again shifted away from exchange toward persuasion, I came back at him with a twenty percent serious Buddhist conversion pitch and he listened graciously. In the ensuing conversation, I explained (one hundred percent seriously) the core aspects of my beliefs.

The next time we spoke in private was when the impromptu coffee gathering at the Plaza Restaurant broke up well before the time when Pam was to pick Larry up to return to the farm. I suggested he call where she was working and ask her to pick him up at my place. He seemed grateful to escape the gray noise of the diner and touched by a simple act of friendship.

[He had followers and acquaintances, but I doubt that he had many friends.]

Apparently, Larry felt emboldened. Sitting at my kitchen table, he explained the foundations of his beliefs.

[Was it a moment of weakness or did he see it as a strategic opportunity?]

He began awkwardly and hesitantly in the manner of someone making a socially risky disclosure, but as he spoke, his aura of conviction and urgency grew. He believed that a secret society of Jewish bankers was poised to take over the world. Mounted cavalry from Russia and China were already hidden away in American national forests and wilderness areas awaiting the order to burn, pillage, and rape as they swarmed out across America and reduced her to utter subservience. This would be a prelude to the apocalypse. He said with measured reverence and not a trace of irony that he knew this because he had been told by God in a series of visions that were foretold in scripture. His explanations of complex webs of minute scriptural implications were filled with the complex logic of delusion that invariably arises when one begins reasoning with a conclusion rather than a question.

The obvious implication implicit in Larry's revelation was that if it was a prophecy foretold in scripture, then he, Larry Hill, was a prophet. He had just declared himself to be a prophet of Biblical proportions without a trace of irony. He truly believed what he was saying.

[To be fair, he never directly called himself a "prophet."]

I had to consciously contain my gasp. It was like getting up in the morning and finding a rattlesnake in my living room.

[We're not in eccentricity anymore, Toto.]

I said, "Well, I think it's pretty obvious that the current social system isn't sustainable, but I'm more inclined to expect a slow crumbling than a sudden collapse. It'll happen on nature's pace, not ours."

[I had no inclination to give much effort to the refutation of a self-evident absurdity.]

And then Pam arrived to pick him up.

Regardless of whatever other kinks you carry, a firm belief in Armageddon's imminence will make you functionally a psychopath in dangerous ways.

A person who is urgently preparing for the sudden, complete, and violent unraveling of civil society and trying desperately to enable those they love and the living word of their God to survive is a very dangerous person. Their belief system has been fully weaponized. Anyone who, whether intentionally or by happenstance, interferes with the necessary preparations will have big ugly bull's-eyes on their heart and back.

[Genuine belief in imminent apocalypse would give permission to ideas and behaviors that would be variously absurd, unthinkable, and/or wrong in normal times]

It's one thing to embrace a spiritual tradition that includes the idea of some sort of final judgment or even Valhalla; it's quite another to see Armageddon as something as imminent and certain as next year's taxes. I can't pretend to offer a meaningful clinical or social diagnosis, but for the sake of pragmatism in steering my daily life, "fucking nuts" is descriptively accurate enough for my decision(s) about whom I want to associate with socially.

[I don't like hanging out with people who dwell in utter certainty about the nature and meaning of the world. I find them moderately frightening and deeply boring.]

We never visited the farm again. On a few occasions, I encountered one or another of the women in town. They always smiled and said, "hello." I don't recall when I noticed that I hadn't seen anyone from Windy Ridge Farm in a long time and, not long afterward, drove by the farm on the way to a hike. It was unoccupied.

[When the jolt of fear precipitated by Larry's tale of divine revelations and holy war gradually subsided, his delusions became merely poignant. I felt a puzzled fondness for those people and wished them well—they carried a load of belief that would weigh anyone down in a hard way.]

I ripped two-by-fours down the middle for material to frame two four-by-eight foot sheets of luan into rigidity and stood them side-by-side against the back wall of the studio to form a large working space where I could tack paper or canvas and pace around the room as I worked. Large amounts of acrylic paints were applied with artist's brushes, cheap wall painting brushes, foam applicators, palette knives, and putty knives while wetting and rewetting the surfaces with an atomizer. Diluted paint ran down the painting wall, through the floor, and streaked the basement wall with color.

In the summer of 1987, a large Paul Klee retrospective came to the Cleveland Museum of Art. Terry, Holly, Oren, and I spent a weekend with Stan, an old college friend, and his wife, Cheryl, and we all traveled north to Cleveland for a day.

[Stan was teaching at Wooster College.]

At the museum, I thought Oren, who was four years old, would be more interested in swords and suits of armor than in paintings, but he was captivated by the Klee exhibition and cried when we had to leave.

Seeing so much of Klee's work all together confirmed and expanded my growing sense of the cumulative value of a life's work and of the way my own paintings constituted a kind of journal that flowed forth from the confluence of emotion and perception. The exhibition revived a long chain of past epiphanies and renewed my faith in the necessity and vitality of art.

But that weekend with Stan and Cheryl had a pivotal importance beyond the rekindling of artistic passion. I was starved for the kind of free-ranging, openly speculative, intellectual conversation that was Stan's forte. We caught up on each other's lives, shared thoughts on books, films, music, art, and politics, and reminisced about the Clarion University hippie days when our lives had first converged.

Stan's life as a teacher, though not without its drudgeries and frustrations, had an abundance of much that I was getting as a bare subsistence ration in my life as a bureaucrat. He told of his own frustrations when, after he left Clarion, Pennsylvania, he was offered a job in educational television in West Virginia. He accepted the position with eager, youthful idealism, fueling intentions and expectations of doing good and noble work. He quickly discovered that he had, in fact, taken a job as a bureaucrat. He sank into a deep, chronic funk of disillusionment.

Stan said, "My routine was to work and come home to a small cockroach-infested trailer (could never get rid of them no matter how I tried) where I would sit and drink six packs of three-two beer, smoke bowl after bowl of cheap local homegrown pot, and watch old TV shows until I finally passed out. My epiphany came one evening when a rerun of the TV series "Gomer Pyle USMC" was pre-empted by some major news story. I don't remember what... some international crisis, assassination... the details are long lost and unimportant. The salient thing was that I had this sudden moment in which I observed myself and found that I was experiencing actual grief, profound sadness, a real palpable sense of loss, almost to tears, as if someone close to me had died, over the interruption, the loss of a Gomer Pyle rerun. It was like waking up inside a Twilight Zone episode. It was a moment of full-on existential terror. It was an almost Zen moment of enlightenment. I felt like I could leave the meditation chamber and run to the front of the temple and ring the giant bell, to announce in no uncertain terms, that I had gotten IT. It was like being lost in some subterranean cavern and suddenly seeing the faintest low glimmer of light pointing a path to the surface. I needed to go back, back to Clarion and back to the university and finish the bachelors degree and start over."

"The horror, the horror," I said with mock gravity. We laughed and passed the pipe.

Stan's Gomer Pyle, cheap beer, and West Virginia weed epiphany became my own.

On my first workday after our Ohio trip, Oren begged me not to go to work and cried when I left.

July 22, 1987: When I arrived home from the office yesterday, (Oren was asleep—he's ill—Holly was away) Terry knelt before me, and when our bodies pulsed and rippled in perfect ecstatic harmony, she turned her eyes up to meet mine, and we slid to the floor in a rushing flood of kisses.

The Daylight Zone

In the spring, a month before he turned eleven, my son Oren and I went camping at a small, unattended campground in the Allegheny National Forest near the confluence of Minister Creek and the much larger Tionesta Creek.

Though the campground was otherwise empty, a group of perhaps a half-dozen younger people (I didn't count) was camped outside the campground, a hundred yards downstream toward the Tionesta. We pitched our tent, gathered some firewood, and went stump shooting with our longbows.

We shot blunt-tipped arrows at sticks and stumps—the first one to hit the designated target chose the next target and shot last. Longbows have a built in safety factor by virtue of their limited range, but it's still best not to intrude upon people doing other things—playing with weapons in close proximity to strangers is simply rude.

Giving the campers a wide berth, we didn't do any shooting until we were well out away from them in the open woods of the valley bottom. Birds, squirrels, and chipmunks were abundant and active. Bright sunlight filtered through a not very dense leafy canopy. Our conversation rambled pleasantly as we meandered around the forested flood plain following our arrows. It was a memorably idyllic day.

With a longbow, there is no mechanical shortcut to accuracy—one must learn to feel the bow as an extension of one's body and then practice until it becomes as intuitive as throwing a ball. In the early days of learning to shoot a bow, the breakthroughs feel almost magical, the arrow seemingly guided as much by the mind as by eyes and arms. Oren had lately achieved a breakthrough in his shooting and enjoyed his newfound prowess exuberantly.

Our wandering took us to a small inlet formed by millennia of Tionesta floodwaters. On the sandbar that rimmed the upstream edge of the inlet there was a section of saw-cut log thirty inches in diameter and thirty inches high standing on end. Probably left there by spring floodwaters, it was waterlogged, but not rotten and much too hard to shoot without breaking our arrows. I stepped up onto it briefly to see if the additional height would yield a better downstream view.

We followed our arrows a bit farther downstream along the Tionesta and then returned by the same route intent on dinner and a campfire. When we arrived back at the sandbar, less than a half-hour after we were first there, the log was gone. Its imprint on the sand was visible, but there were no drag marks, and we saw no footprints, other than our own. I don't know how much the log weighed, but I doubt that I could have moved it and I certainly couldn't have picked it up. The log's disappearance was, in a sense, a very small, mundane event. It was also a very genuine mystery.

On our way back to camp, the other campers were gathered at their unofficial site cooking dinner. We neither saw nor heard a sign of anyone else.

The true mysteries in my life have all been like that—no trace of drama, no cinematic paranormal spookiness, but rather, perfect blends of the surreal and the banal situated not in the twilight zone, but in broad daylight.

The surreal and the banal are not nearly as different as most of us would prefer to believe.

That's an Order

When I discovered one of the caseworkers I supervised was investigating his clients far beyond the Pennsylvania Department of Public Welfare's procedural requirements for verification, I objected for several reasons. The most obvious and basic reason was that his clients were being subjected to greater scrutiny than others, i.e. discrimination based not on race, religion, or sexual orientation, but on the luck of the draw when caseworkers were assigned. Though some procedural inconsistency was inevitable due to variations in the personalities and competence of caseworkers, it was limited on the anal-retentive zealotry end of the scale by policy, procedure, and workload, and on the incompetent end of the scale by supervision and performance evaluations.

[At least theoretically.]

But this situation was larger than uniformity and competence. Providing verification rightfully belonged to the applicant or recipient as a fundamental responsibility. Requiring recipients to take that responsibility was neither punitive nor naïve; rather it was a matter of ensuring that they fully engaged this process in their lives just as they would have to engage other processes in their lives in order to regain their self-sufficiency. The caseworker's job was to assist them if they hit a snag, not to prowl the underbrush and pounce on the walking wounded. Many of our clients had already been pounced upon, in one way or another, rather too much in their lives. Besides, our county was burdened with excessive caseloads, and time spent chasing any procedural issue beyond legal requirements could only result in unmet needs somewhere else in the process.

I asked the caseworker to cut it out, to simply follow the procedure manual and let it go.

[I hated giving direct orders to adults. I'm not all that comfortable giving orders to children. I'm okay with well-trained dogs.

Life at the office seemed much better if I could say, "Could you do this for me?" And the caseworker said, "Sure," and I replied, "Thank you." Or the caseworker could say, "Yes, but there could be a problem because...." That was my management style. Everyone knew that my request was, in essence, an order. Delivering the order with a built-in expression of gratitude and an opening for the expression of misgivings was more than just being polite; it was a vital courtesy that smoothed the abrasive arbitrariness of authority.]

The caseworker argued that the department's verification requirements ought to be more stringent. I said, "First of all, that's a legislative issue, not a frontline administrative one, and second, when your supervisor tells you that you don't have to work as hard anymore, the appropriate response is to smile and say 'Thank you'."

Two weeks later, I learned that the caseworker had continued to conduct his vigilante investigations. When I confronted him and reiterated that he was to meet procedural requirements and go no further, he said, "I just don't see why I have to do it that way."

"What's your job title?"

"Caseworker."

"What's my job title?"

"Casework Supervisor."

"You got it, my man! That's why you have to do it that way."

Most of the people in my unit were better caseworkers than I had ever been or had even tried to be. They knew this, and so did I. Some were insightfully calm enough to recognize that I was a better supervisor than I was a caseworker, that the two positions required different strengths and could accommodate different weaknesses. Some saw my promotion as undeserved in light of their own obviously greater competence and so they resented my authority, even though they hadn't applied for the position. Their bitterness was mostly their own problem, because my ego wasn't heavily engaged. I hadn't felt uniquely qualified for the promotion.

*[I had applied for the supervisor position mainly because I was afraid someone ambitious and anal retentive would apply and become **my** supervisor.]*

Wielding authority felt uncomfortable and exhausting, so I preferred not to wield it. The courtesies I employed mostly served to protect me from the exhaustion of exercising authority, so I could go home at the end of the day with sufficient emotional reserves to be a decent parent, husband, and artist.

[I preferred not to ever have to fire anyone.]

Gilbert's Shadow

Gilbert gave us moments, and sometimes hour-long torrents, of impossibly rich and deeply nuanced understanding that many of us had been unsure were even truly possible, until then. He could only give these scattered moments and occasional hours because the extraordinary man he once was had long ago drowned in a synapse-killing flood of whisky. He would rush harried, hurried, and a few minutes late into his Shakespeare class and deliver a jaw droppingly brilliant, hour-long, extemporaneous lecture on Faulkner, Fitzgerald, or Joyce. When the class ended, the science and business majors would scratch their heads and exchange lame sarcasms, while the artists and English majors headed for a bar, embroiled in conversation already wandering farther afield than Gilbert's misdirected soliloquy. We were so starved for brilliance that Gilbert's fleeting flourishes of genius consigned the other moments of blundering, alcoholic stupor to a barely remembered background and effectively camouflaged the pitiful, besotted poignancy of the wreck he had become. We were so enamored of our own newfound wildness that we saw only a reflection of our dissident liberation in the shiny surface of his disintegration.

[Bear was a medium-sized, black mongrel stray, who had been adopted as a sort of mascot by the hippie community. If he stopped by the student union in mid-afternoon someone would always buy him a hamburger or a hotdog. Bear knew where all the hippies lived and made his rounds visiting. He would scratch at the front door and be welcomed in to hang out for a while and get high before

moving on for reasons known only to him. He loved to have marijuana smoke blown in his face. People gave Bear acid regularly. His eyes were radiantly gentle when he was tripping.]

The English department organized an outdoor poetry reading. Gilbert, as the possessor of Clarion's closest thing to literary renown, was the featured poet, to be followed by other faculty members and the college president's son-in-law. When Gilbert stepped unsteadily to the podium and began to speak, Bear approached him barking loudly. Gilbert began barking back at him and got down on all fours. Bear and Gilbert circled each other on the sunny lawn, barking and growling. The audience laughed nervously. I slipped away and walked to the Longhorn Bar, where I ordered a pitcher of beer and sat in a dim back corner, alone.

After Gilbert died, Al (a friend and colleague who taught sculpture at the university) went to the house to check on Gilbert's widow and found her in the backyard, deep in drunken despondency, throwing handfuls of paper into a fire. A fragment blew free from the flames and landed at Al's feet. It was a fragment of a letter to Gilbert signed by Man Ray. Al snatched what he could from the fire and did his best to calm and comfort the distraught widow.

[When I saw Al a few days later, his hands and forearms were bandaged.]

She gave him the bundle of papers she had been feeding a handful at a time to the fire. It was a treasure trove. There were letters and drawings from Man Ray, Henry Miller, F. Scott Fitzgerald, Paul Eluard, Anais Nin, Alan Watts, Jack Kerouac, Allen Ginsburg, John Steinbeck, and others.

We all knew Gilbert had a personal history interwoven with the veritable deities of our intellectual heritage. We didn't realize until much later that the distance our awe created only deepened his lonely tragedy. If we had been braver, more self-contained in our own brilliance, perhaps his decline might have been less lonely even though, by then, most of the damage to his psyche and liver had already been done.

Our failure to see the agony of Gilbert's gushing psychic wound points an accusing finger, like a Shakespearean ghost and indicts the shallow enlightenment of the sixties. I have no decent explanation for our ability to witness his vast, radiant pain with such deficient empathy. We took more than we gave. Though it sounds maudlin and lame, someone should have hugged Gilbert and thanked him. We couldn't have saved him. I don't even know what "saving him" could have meant, but perhaps we could have saved ourselves, at least a little.

[Decades later, the same spiritual failure blossomed into absurd war. Much of the generation that dedicated its youthful outrage and exuberance to the cause of peace turned narrow, savage, and viciously self-righteous.]

Integration in 1971

In his new job in North Carolina, my father was the maintenance manager for a manufacturer of power tools. When he was told that there would be separate Christmas parties for white and "colored" employees, Clyde informed the next higher level of management, which included the old friend who had recruited him for the job, that everyone from the maintenance department would attend the same party—they simply needed to know which one that should be.

He did this with full support from the people who worked for him—blacks, whites, and even a Klan member he described as a "beady-eyed little shithead."

[These men were more united by their labor than divided by their race.]

The entire factory's Christmas party was matter-of-factly integrated for the first time.

The Metaphysics of Equality

Part One

In the summer of 1982, Jack, an old college friend and fellow welfare caseworker, stopped by on his way home from a workshop with Ram Dass at Omega Institute. During the workshop, Ram Dass told the group that he had invited someone who was conducting another workshop at Omega to speak to them. He introduced Oren Lyons, a Faithkeeper of the Turtle Clan of the Onondaga Nation. A fellow participant in the workshop recorded the talk (with permission) and gave Jack a copy, which he then played and copied for me and my wife, Terry.

Lyons spoke with the clarity, directness, and simplicity of truly fundamental wisdom. He spoke what I already knew, but hadn't known how to articulate, even to myself.

[When our son was born the following summer, we named him "Oren."]

My thoughts have wandered back to various aspects of that talk many times in the intervening years, but one small, resonant gem in particular has resurfaced again and again: "All life is equal."

I'm not going to attempt a treatise elucidating the vast territory of implication contained in that statement—I'm too old for such torture and lack patience for the public recitation of analytic minutiae.

[I'll try to keep it simple for my own sake.]

Though I'm not a poet, the vividness of truth I seek has more to do with poetics than philosophy and often resides not in my words, but in the territory beyond them.

[Occasionally, I blunder into something best rendered in verse.]

What shakes my brain is the way that simple four-word sentence dovetails with one of my core beliefs.

[Distilled from Buddhism.]

There is no necessary logical correlation between belief in an afterlife and theism. There could quite possibly be a god and still no afterlife, and there could just as easily be an afterlife and no god. Theism and afterlife are entirely separate issues. Personally, I can see karma at work in the world, but the Grand Spook eludes me.

[Though I'm interested in where other ideas wander, debate about such things often seems like a waste of life.]

So here's what seems likely to me:

[Likelihood is as close as I can get to belief and it usually seems close enough.]

The body, the whole thing, including the brain, is a sense organ, or a sensory array, if you will. The spiritual difference between a human and a cat, horse, deer, dog, crow, vulture, shark, butterfly, snake, insect, oak tree, cactus, lichen, etcetera is merely a matter of sensory equipment. The nature of the underlying consciousness is the same. The sensory/biological array (the body) is a fruit that ripens, falls, and rots. The new array that regrows after the old one drops back to the Earth is shaped by complex karma. That's roughly how it works and it doesn't matter much whether there's a god peering through the keyhole when it all goes down. It just happens like gravity, sedimentation, old age, and fire.

[The intellectual violence of dogma fills me with fear and angst.]

Part Two

If this flesh is merely the fruiting body/sensory array of a larger, broader, or simply more primal being, there is no a priori or logical reason to assume that the submerged four-fifths of the metaphorical bloody iceberg couldn't bear more than one fruit.

How many?

Two, eight, ten thousand? I realize you can march that number right up to absurd infinity and God, but it all gets seriously meaningless long before you get there.

[Reductio ad absurdum.]

Let's just grant that there could be maybe two, maybe twenty (one for each finger and toe); something at least comprehensively finite. Do we sometimes meet the mysterious fruit of our own being? Do we sometimes give birth to it? Kill it? Make love with it?

[Etcetera ad absurdum.]

Sometimes, even if only for a moment, we wordlessly recognize a profound kinship with another being.

[Sometimes human, sometimes not—it's way more complicated than blood.]

Perhaps we blossom and fruit in more than one world.

[This probably has more to do with quantum physics than philosophy.]

The mystery exceeds the reach and grasp of both belief and reason.

[This is not a problem.]

Part Three

On a bright summer day, an immature male rose-breasted grosbeak collided with our sunroom window directly in front of me.

[The thud of a bird on a window is a special, poignant kind of ugly.]

I went out expecting to find the fallen bird dead, but he laid belly up on the drip edge gravel, breathing. It was the time of day when the sun beats directly down on our forest edge backyard, and the gravel was hot to the touch.

[It seemed like a terrible place to die.]

I gently picked up the young grosbeak intending to take him to the shade of a nearby lilac and sit with him to keep other creatures away, but he visibly revived in my hands. He turned his head to look around and moved his feet tentatively. I carefully examined his wings and felt no broken bones.

Very conscious and aware now, the bird didn't seem fearful in the least.

[Yes, I'm being anthropomorphic.]

I turned him over and he stood up. I spoke softly and lightly stroked his head with my finger.

[A glimmer of hope rising.]

I reached out to a low-hanging spruce branch, and the young bird walked the length of my fingers to step onto it. After a few minutes, he flew away into the woods.

Welfare and Wildness in Happy Valley

When Wade was promoted from caseworker to casework supervisor, he created the caseworker vacancy I was hired to fill when I transferred in from another county. Wade's personal wildness electrified the air around him. To like him, one had to be sufficiently open, bright, and subtle to perceive and value the gentleness and integrity lurking behind his twinkling eyes and profanity.

January 6, 1978: Beauty is made of tiny ghosts; the rest is television and metal and good intentions that don't matter much.

I was in Wade's office discussing a case and playing fussball when another caseworker came in.

[Wade had a fussball table and a dartboard in his office. A dart or fussball game lightened the atmosphere around a difficult conversation and allowed Wade to wield authority without being authoritarian.]

"My eleven o'clock wants an emergency check, and I don't think we should give it to him."

"Why not?"

"He'll just spend it on drugs."

"Yeah, probably—I know him—he's a fucking junkie. How does he look?"

"Sweating like a pig and fidgety as hell."

"I'll go take a look. You take over," Wade said as he gestured toward the handles on his side of the fussball table and exited the room.

Wade returned in a few minutes and asked, "Is he eligible?"

"Yeah."

"Well, he's hurting, and I don't give a shit what he spends his money on. If you want to make people who are hurting hurt even worse, you're in the wrong job. Give him his fucking check."

The caseworker said, "Okay," sighed, and walked out.

"Damn, he even fucked up the game—I'm behind now."

"That's the only way I'm ever going to beat you, Wade."

March 16, 1978: The office is weirdly silent—background murmur composed of low voices and the scratch of pens. Yearnings both nameless and named and a constant awareness of a day's cruel brevity, while unwanted snow falls past the office windows. On and on—so existential it's almost parody. Neck deep in over-determination, I would rather believe in fate, but can't. Nothing, not even the snow or wind seems simple or even innocent today.

I should be in the woods—follow a fox track, watch hawks, eat snow…

Like poverty, prolonged, stress-ridden drudgery atrophies one's sense of delayed gratification. When you have fifteen minutes left in your lunch hour, you have another beer and when the good-looking female coworker you have nothing in common with wants to give you a blowjob at the office picnic, you do it.

May 31, 1978: Can my hands make mirrors for my spirit?
Biomorphs.
Spaceful flatness (color).
Waiting and hunger.
Light (surface).
Mired in procrastinated necessity—energized in smoke clouds and teacups.
Cruising into painted action wearing a job like lead shoes. If that's what patience and discipline are all about, dare anyone call it virtue? It's my life, and all this impedimentia must be a part of me, somehow—along with my written desperation and my spoken while grinning sarcasms.

A cross match with the Social Security computer system turned up nearly a year of unreported wages for one of my clients. After obtaining the appropriate documentation from the employer, I completed an overpayment report recommending prosecution for fraud and sent a letter to the client notifying her of the pending prosecution and the discontinuance of her benefits.

The angry, agitated woman telephoned immediately upon receiving the letter. She demanded an explanation, but wouldn't pause from her ranting flurry of outrage, denial, and profanity long enough for me to offer one or even point out that instructions for filing an appeal were included in the letter. Since she was literally screaming into the phone, her rant was fully audible to caseworkers at nearby desks.

[I sat in a large open space containing desks for more than twenty caseworkers. There were no cubicles.]

Someone alerted Wade, and he was already standing beside me when the woman demanded to speak to my supervisor.

[Let's call her Mrs. Doe.]

"Mr. Darling says he recommended prosecution for fraud. Just what the hell is that supposed to mean?"

"That means you're in deep shit, Mrs. Doe."

A renewed torrent of rage and profanity spewed forth from the telephone. Wade rolled his eyes back and dangled his tongue out the side of his mouth. He held the receiver to his crotch and began doing theatrical bumps and grinds against it, while moaning softly. The other caseworkers in the room were variously amused and/or aghast.

After a few minutes, Mrs. Doe finally depleted her fury and hung up.

"Fucking lying piece of shit," Wade muttered as he walked away.

July 12, 1978: Awake and clear at 6:30, despite last night's excess of beer. Looked at current paintings, read Fowles, and suddenly, I'm behind my gray steel desk locked into a long day's rationed procrastination. (The times that are my own, escape so fast.)

So many words, yet so few.

Cool air sun.

Cumulus clouds.

Interviews.

Wait, want.

Idle temptations.

Visual meaning—you have to start by clarifying what that is—the poignancy, stress, angst, joy, confusion, clarity, love, time, and motion that can so gracefully inhabit a form, a few lines, or a splash of color—how does that originate? That's the question.

Perception itself has to be clarified—revisions in its content are simply not enough to distinguish art from any other mode of social conditioning.

As I write, Bill and Harry come to my desk to talk business. Behind them sits Olivia who catches my eye and makes a subtle, but definite show of masturbating beneath her desk, while maintaining eye contact. I am uncomfortably and involuntarily aroused (remembering a quick, surreptitious office picnic blowjob).

Then the receptionist informed me that a client was here to see me. In the reception area I find a woman three years younger than I, but seeming so much older. After I got the information I needed from the hard luck woman, I returned to my desk, and sexual tension hung in the air, like the smoke of our smoldering collective boredom.

The intake supervisor described Saul as "the dirtiest human being in Pennsylvania." It may have been true. He looked like a coal miner at the end of a workday and smelled like a well-aged blend of fuel oil and cat shit. But Saul wasn't hard to get along with. All you had to do was endure the stench, ignore the dead flies and rotting food in his beard, and wash your pen after he used it to sign papers.

August 7, 1978: The weekend started fine and turned crazy. I painted with renewed energy and basked in the glow of good work, until Sunday afternoon when there was an outdoor farewell party for a departing co-worker. Wade got very loaded—much too loaded (Quaalude, Dexedrine, weed, and beer) and got vulgarly and loudly aggressive toward Maria, with whom he is secretly and painfully in love. She's married. I have rather a crush on her too—she's extraordinary—but it's not painful because all my painful spots are already occupied by other women. I tried to defuse the situation, but he was so crazily persistent, he didn't back off until I threatened him physically. He didn't have to come back down too far to make apologies and ask forgiveness, and then I drank way too much.

Sleep came hard, and Monday morning came gray and sick. My somber indifference mirrors the rainy sky. Waiting for the sun.

There was an open caseworker position, but the director hadn't requested a civil service list. A recent hiring freeze could get reinstated at any moment. I had a talk with Wade about Bea, with whom my longtime on again/off again relationship was in an on phase. Bea was a caseworker in another county and wanted to transfer. The director wasn't in his office, but we knew where to find him. He was at the Sheraton, sitting alone at the bar. Wade took a stool on one side of him. I took a stool on the other. He glanced back and forth at us with an expression of mock disgust and said, "What do I have to do to get a little peace? Do I have to go home and drink; is that what you want me to do?" Then he ordered beers for both of us.

Wade said, "We have a caseworker who wants to transfer in from another county, but you've gotta act on it right away."

"Which one of you is fucking her?"

"Not me," Wade replied.

The director turned, looked at me, and said, "This better be worth it."

"The caseloads are out of control," I said.

"So is Wade."

"That's your problem."

"No, it's your problem too."

"You have a point there," I said as I raised my glass to tap his in a toast.

"I'll get on it in the morning."

March 12, 1979: I socialize too much with bureaucrats and absorb an excess of their negative energies. They tend to lack any real aspirations beyond coping with the stress and strangeness of their vocation. For most of them, that seems to be enough, but for me, it is despair.

When Rich transferred in from another county there was visible tension between him and Ozzie from the beginning, but the mutual abrasion was stupidly and comfortably petty on both sides and enveloped in enough distraction to prevent a collision. Both were Vietnam vets who bore visible scars that surely had invisible counterparts.

[Ozzie's from a landmine, and Rich's from a Vietcong bayonet.]

Ozzie was in a different supervisory unit, but he liked to join Wade's unit, which included Rich and me, when we gathered at a country tavern in Pleasant Gap for lunch, beer, laughter, and wild talk. Wade was the gonzo supervisor and we were the gonzo unit in the welfare office—outrageous, outspoken, incorrigible, and smart enough to get away with it.

[There was strange darkness in our laughter.]

Today it was different. Joints were passed en route, and pitchers of beer came and went at a crazy pace while we ranted and laughed—that much was normal, but Ozzie had the proverbial bug up his ass. He prodded and insulted Rich repeatedly. Rich shrugged it off at first, but I could see something rising in him that I knew only too well in myself—he was beginning to *want* Ozzie to push things too far. Wade saw it too and said "I can't watch this shit," as he got up to leave.

Rich, well aware of his own sharp edges and tender buttons, kept his temper in check, until Ozzie said something that he interpreted as threatening to his family. Rich set his beer glass down on the bar, turned to Ozzie, and said, "Okay, let's go outside and settle this."

[Rich had six children and was a devoted father wrestling uncomfortably with his own inveterate wildness.]

Ozzie smiled, rubbed his palms together, and said, "This is just what I've been waiting for!"

Ozzie was over six feet tall and rail thin. I doubt that he weighed a hundred-fifty pounds. Rich was over six feet tall and built like the football player he had been in college.

They hustled outside where Ozzie did his best rendition of a yell from a cheap martial arts movie and assumed his version of a karate master's fighting stance. Rich seized him by the shoulders, slammed his head against the side of the brick building, threw him on the ground, and returned to the bar.

As Rich reached for the beer pitcher, Ozzie came in the front door, yelled wildly, and leaped through the air in a surprisingly athletic and faithful rendition of a barroom brawl scene from an old John Wayne movie. He missed, and as he sailed past, Rich grabbed him and threw him through the ladies' room door. Ozzie bounced off the wall and landed with his shoulders wedged between the wall and the toilet. Rich strode across the bar to the small ladies room and, as Ozzie's legs flailed wildly in a frantic effort to extricate himself, punched him repeatedly, until we led Rich away and out, while frantically apologizing to the bartender.

As the fight was erupting, Wade missed a curve on the mountain road to his home and slammed into a cliff face totaling his car. Another caseworker, who lived nearby, found Wade standing in the road next to the wreckage, spitting out pieces of windshield glass and cursing.

Neither Ozzie nor Rich pressed charges. Ozzie readily forgave Rich and blamed Wade for the whole incident. Though far from rational, this wasn't entirely unfounded. Wade had an aura that jacked up the emotional energy in any situation—it seemed hard wired. He was incapable of not doing it and when he was cranked, it could be good, sometimes extraordinarily good, and always better than the background buzz of welfare bureaucracy's stagnant tragedy. In the wake of his beating, Ozzie reacted to Wade's wild charisma as if it was a conspiracy directed at him. The coke Ozzie snorted in the men's room didn't help at all.

[The tavern owner banned all caseworkers from the premises.]
Since we feared Ozzie might be teetering on the brink of an even higher cliff, I became Wade's bodyguard for a few weeks.

***March 25, 1979:** Must one sacrifice transcendence in order to attain comfort?*

As I walked past Ozzie's desk, he hissed like a reptile and sprang out of his chair. I reflexively pivoted and drew back my fist, ready to punch him as he collapsed on the floor in a seizure. Many heads bobbed up from the rows of caseworkers' desks in time to see my aborted punch. Acutely aware of the eyes upon me, I ducked into Wade's office.

[Ozzie was epileptic as a result of his war injuries. The coke he snorted in the men's room didn't help with that, either.]
"Ozzie is having a seizure—I hope someone out there is helping him because I can't do it."

"He can fucking die as far as I'm concerned," Wade said as he went to the door to make sure someone was, indeed, helping Ozzie.

***March 28, 1979:** Phillipsburg office—an old lady wanting more food stamps, an anxious, not very bright young woman who told me, "the doctor says my baby's head is growing too fast," and that her husband beats her up, an old man dying of a heart condition, a senile old lady who doesn't know what she wants and can't hear because she won't remove her furry winter hat even though its forty-seven degrees outside, and an about to be evicted, fat ugly, angry, pregnant young woman for whom I can do nothing.*

The intake unit's casework supervisor, a pathetic, cynical wreck of a human being whose spirit had foundered on decades of morale-crushing work and a marriage gone hopelessly bitter, walked over to Bea's desk, threw a case record folder down in front of her, and said, "That's the stupidest goddamned thing I've ever seen." He then proceeded to loudly berate her work performance in front of the entire casework staff. She was in tears. As soon as he turned to walk away, I went to her desk and said, "I'm speaking now as a union steward, not as a friend. Do you want to file a grievance?"

"No, I just want to forget it."

"You won't be able to forget it, because it has happened to others before and it'll happen again. That scene was extremely unpleasant for everyone, not just you."

"I don't want to do it."

Though I wasn't contractually required to obtain an employee's consent to file a grievance on their behalf, I reluctantly let it go in the name of domestic harmony.

A week later, I was conferring with a clerk and another caseworker about a case situation, when the intake supervisor interrupted with a case record folder in his hand, "The client is in the reception area—go take this application." I was not on intake, he was not my assigned supervisor, there was no emergency situation, and no one from the intake staff had called in sick.

I said, "No, Mr. Calder, I won't take that case," in a calm voice.

Already getting red-faced, he said, "Are you refusing a direct order?"

"Yes, Mr. Calder, I am."

"You can be disciplined for this," he said in a loud angry voice.

I smiled and said, "You're welcome to try."

He roared into a blustery, profanity-laden rant.

I filed a class action grievance on behalf of the entire casework staff, named Bea and myself as the two specifically aggrieved parties, and cited both incidents as examples of verbal abuse and violation of employee confidentiality. The director was in Harrisburg for two days of meetings.

At home that evening, I walked out of a raging, tear-flooded argument with Bea and returned late and drunk. She left the next morning on a six-day vacation with a group of friends.

When the director returned, he summoned Wade and me to his office. Wade said, "I had a unit meeting and ordered all my people to refuse work assignments from that fat, fucking piece of shit." The director sighed and said, "I'll take care of it."

Though there was little doubt that I was contractually right, and that Calder had attempted to assign work punitively, it was equally transparent that I had deliberately provoked him.

Calder was ordered to conduct all performance or behavior related conferences with courtesy and respect, in the privacy of his office and to channel any intake work that couldn't be handled by the intake unit through his fellow supervisors.

My self-righteousness faded with my anger.

May 10, 1979: Watching misty moonlight from my bedroom window.
Bird sounds punctuate the body's call to sleep.
Time.

On "Gentle Thursday," an annual, hippie-esque celebration of spring and peace on a Penn State lawn, an assortment of people from the welfare office gathered on a couple of blankets to hang out in warm spring sun, drink beer, listen to music, and talk.

The group was mostly female, plus Ozzie, Earl from the Department of Agriculture office next door, and me. Ozzie began to hold forth about his mastery of martial arts.

"You would have to have a gun to touch me," he said. I picked up an orange in my right hand, held it out at arm's length, and tossed it lightly up and caught it a few times. Then I quickly shot my left hand out to my side and wiggled my fingers. When Ozzie looked at my left hand, I threw the orange and hit him in the groin.

There was a flash of fire in Ozzie's eyes. One of the women gasped, and another muttered, "Oh shit." I picked up my beer and said, "Cheers."

Ozzie smiled and said, "Good one!"

I invited Ozzie to smoke a joint on the top level of the Pugh Street parking garage. On the way there, he told me that women found him irresistible because his penis was ten inches long. I replied in my best mock-pious tone, "Oh, you must feel so very blessed."

Ozzie said, "You know, you can be a real asshole sometimes."

"Yeah, I've noticed that about myself."

July 4, 1979: Somber, daylong rain—the sun came out just in time to set, and I painted on, taking breaks for chores, joints, and raspberry picking— quietly wordless all day—channeling my attention through my brush with a mixture of diligence and escapism.

Now, writing in my solitary bed, I listen to the sounds of distant dogs, cars, and the wind.

Ozzie stepped back from his brink, fell in love, and seemed to settle back toward sanity. He became a not unpleasant coworker, but I kept my distance socially.

August 19, 1979: Night comes dense, moist, and filled with cricket song. Far away lightning flashes behind the fog. Silence is chewed ragged at its edges by distant engines, while I ponder, wonder, and regret.

Six years later, Rich was killed in a car accident. Ozzie was eventually promoted to casework supervisor. He married, had children, and died young of lung cancer.

November 19, 1979: On the phone, a screaming client who wouldn't take "no" on a car purchase grant and said he was "coming down there to get it or else." So he came in, big and irate, and I talked him down and sent him on his grumbling way.

The hard part is the anticipation—knowing you have to go out there and deal with a boatload of irrational anger agitates the psyche in a way that takes all day to smooth back out.

The director came to Wade's office looking stressed, "The auditors are eating us alive—why is this happening?" he asked.

"It's because we're incompetent," Wade replied.

Rattlesnakes and Rain

Early in my eighteenth autumn, I backpacked upstream along the Tionesta Creek from Mayburg, Pennsylvania to Logan Run and up Logan Run to its waterfall intending to camp in a small cave in the rock formations uphill from the waterfall, because it seemed like a place of comfort well-suited to pondering and solitude. But when I began gathering kindling for a campfire, I smelled rattlesnakes, and it was not subtle.

I had walked as far as I wanted to that day and had looked forward to settling into the comfort of my little cave, but quickly realized that the indolent ease I needed was not going to be found in a tentless night steeped in the scent of venomous reptiles. I decided to hike southwest, around the head of Phelps Run, into Kingsley Run, which meets the Tionesta Creek at Mayburg. Without navigational errors, this was doable in a couple of hours. I found a comfortable spot on the first bench above the Kingsley Run valley bottom—open and snakeless—without shelter, but the sky was clear. I sat by my little campfire beneath a gloriously starry sky and when the fire burned down to coals, I unrolled my sleeping bag next to it and fell asleep easily.

I was awakened at two a.m. by a ground-shaking crash of thunder, just before the rain arrived in torrential waves. At first, the lightning was so intense that I was able to navigate by its illuminations. When the lightning passed, the flashlight I retrieved from my sodden pack was dead, but by then I was in familiar territory. I arrived at Aunt Gert and Uncle Ed's house a little past three. They welcomed me as if it was perfectly normal to show up unannounced and soaking wet in the middle of the night. I slept in, and Gert cooked a breakfast feast of eggs, bacon, home fries, and toast. Ed told a story of which I remember only the laughter.

Testosterone and Loathing in the Land of Plenty

It's quite understandable that conservatives, especially evangelical Christians, are panicking. They wanted new wallpaper, and these women are tearing out walls.

[It gives them the heebie-jeebies.]

They believe that western culture is splitting apart at the seams and the first seam to go is the crotch of its pants. They're right.

[It doesn't give me the heebie-jeebies.]

They're scared shitless.

[I'm scared too, but not quite shitless.]

Minds are suffocating, and people are being killed.

[I don't want to steal any airtime from women who are speaking up—they are owed plenty of that—but it is incumbent on men to honestly reflect on their own lives and thoughts. This should not happen in secrecy or silence. Substituting male silence for female silence doesn't have a lot of problem-solving potential, even though the women sure could use a break.]

There's a lot I can't pretend to understand—I suspect my personal history is relatively atypical even for my strange generation (the first wave of baby boomers/hippies). I had (and of course, still have) PTSD and chronic depression. My parents gave me this illness. Though they didn't intend to do the kind of lasting damage they did, it isn't like they accidentally sneezed on the salad, either. My father had (officially undiagnosed) PTSD brought home from World War Two and Okinawa, and my mother was deranged—probably a sociopath. I graduated from high school in the summer of love (1967) and began college in the fall. I had a Mensa-level IQ and I was utterly fucking clueless. When the wave that rushed out of Hashbury reached rural Pennsylvania a year later, the personal qualities that had made me a nerd in high school made me attractive in college.

So, if I'm going to speak about even one corner of the multifaceted gawd-awful brutality of gender in the present, I need to begin with full disclosure, because patriarchal culture is an immensely complex fabric woven from countless threads of silence.

[I navigate to relevance intuitively as I search through memory. I apologize in advance for unknown failures.]

From 1968 to 1980, I typically had four or five sexual partners per year—fewer when I was living with a lover, but my monogamy was largely circumstantial. I can't recall a single relationship that began with a conversation about whether we wanted to have sex—not one. At some point, when it was obvious where we were imminently going, I *usually* asked, "Are we safe?" My question was in reference to potential pregnancy.

[The pill was fairly ubiquitous and horrible sexually transmitted diseases were not.]

Attractions were spontaneous and intuitive. There were miscalculations. I can recall a couple of occasions when my kiss/embrace/touch was unwelcome— it wasn't difficult to perceive because desire was what I desired and its absence was powerful. Such moments were searingly embarrassing and my apologies were immediate. I never felt the slightest glimmer of urge to be aggressive. There were also times when I was on the receiving end of unwelcome touch. The women seemed more hurt than embarrassed, and it all just seemed sad. Among the people I tended to hang out with, these blunders were just life, and we gave each other plenty of slack as long as nobody got ornery and nobody got ripped off.

Once in my wandering hippie days when I spent a couple of months with my parents, the wife of one of my father's colleagues took a fancy to me at a party. She was drunk and relentless. When she put her hand on my inner thigh, I leaned in and said in a low voice, "If you don't leave me alone, I'll throw you in the fucking pool." She laughed and failed to comply. I threw her in the pool. Though I have to admit it pretty much ruined the party, I felt completely justified, and my father found it far funnier than he dared admit.

[Her heavily bleached hair turned green from the chlorine.]

I've been outside the world of seeking new sexual and/or romantic relationships since 1980 and I can't claim to have much first-hand knowledge about how the social rituals and protocols of courtship and desire have changed in the past forty years, but surely they have changed. Customs evolve. Amidst those swirling, shifting cultural currents, there is something big and stiff that hasn't changed—male dominance. What collective male dominance requires of individual men is utter subservience to an obsolete inherited barbarism—patriarchal culture's hot, throbbing oxymoron.

My last field interview of the day was scheduled for four o'clock—I got there a few minutes early.

[I didn't like to be late when dealing with so many people who needed to learn how to be on time.]

It was a pretty routine case. My client was a waitress with two kids and no man. She underreported her tips, and I didn't give a shit.

[Republican politicians did and they still do now.]

"Oh, Mr. Darling, I would do anything to keep my food stamps and medical card," she said.

"Well, all you have to do is answer some questions, verify some information, and sign some papers—it's easy."

On the drive home, I realized that in portions of her past and present doing "anything" was the deal by which she and her kids survived.

[There was nothing I could do about that.]

Nowadays, men are scrambling to plea bargain rape down to assault, assault down to boorishness, boorishness down to drunkenness, and drunkenness down to cluelessness in an endless regression of self-doubt that most men are socially forbidden to talk about. The immediate aftermath is not likely to be cool.

[No shit, Sigmund.]

But we have to talk about it. We have to reinvent our culture. It's the only way we can rid ourselves of the pain we have invented, inflicted, and enshrined.

[Failure is not an option.]

The realization men are recoiling from now is that even if they have refrained from sexual aggression not merely as a choice, but also as an ingrained quality of character, even if they have consciously bristled at the visible injustices of sexism for decades, they have engaged in socially toxic behaviors.

I'm not saying that all or most men typically ache with violent lust and/or pathological urges to dominate. I am saying that we've been adrift and clueless in the ubiquitous social conditioning of a patriarchal culture that taught us to behave like assholes as a kind of default setting. Patriarchy has given men as foul a psychological and spiritual fucking over as women. That we got the less constantly painful end of the well-polished turd hasn't been quite as lucky as it might seem.

Most males have engaged in behaviors that exist on a spectrum of behavior that includes rape even though most have never engaged in overt sexual aggression. I think those behaviors cross over the twilight zone between innocence and dominance long before they manifest as overt aggression. This does not make us all de facto rapists, but it does require us to examine, with a mercilessly critical eye, the complex web of social constructs that define our largely unspoken vision of manhood. We have to shed the cluelessness that until now has been our primary absolution.

That's what the breaking of women's silence means: it reduces the complexity, ambiguity, and nuance of complicity to a binary choice. The middle ground has been washed away by a torrent of women's anguished voices. Resistance is the only alternative to complicity.

We need to redefine manhood. This will take a while and the early years will be a real son-of-a-bitch.

Meanwhile, though rigidity tends to be contrary to resiliency, and pontificating has a short half-life in its atomic decay into self-parody, there are a few aspects of the current version that warrant active resistance:

A capacity for histrionic violence seen as manly virtue.

Sex as dominance or conquest.

Power as an intrinsic satisfaction, not merely as a tool.

Willingness to use physical domination and/or implicit physical threats in social

interactions.

Misogyny trivialized by and/or disguised as humor.

Male entitlement to sexual gratification.

Regarding empathy as a weakness (to avoid admitting one is afraid of it).

Zero sum worldview.

[And hey guys, since we're on the subject of toxic masculinity, what's this shit with the assault weapons? We need to have a large, long collective conversation about our violence. You can't deny that the let's-freak-out-and-spray-bullets crew looks a lot like a boy's club.]

Wilbur was crazy—I mean full-blown, potentially dangerous, batshit crazy. Though he thought he was much smarter than he was, he wasn't stupid. The director of the welfare office walked past the reception area just as one of my caseworkers called Wilbur for his application interview. Wilbur's wife remained seated. She radiated an aura of damage.

Wilbur was offended when the caseworker told him his wife's signature would be required on some of the forms, and he demanded to speak to a supervisor—that was me. I said, "Wilbur, your wife is an adult and part of your household. If she is to be included in an assistance grant and a food stamp allotment, she needs to be informed of her rights and responsibilities and sign a paper certifying that she has been thus informed. That's the law. I can't change it."

He went out to the reception area and brought her back to the interview booth. She would not make eye contact, but she answered my questions and signed the papers.

A few minutes after Wilbur left, the director came to my office and said, "I saw Wilbur out there today with his wife—that woman is abused—I would bet on it. There needs to be a home visit."

I said, "I agree, but I'm not comfortable sending one of my people out there alone."

"You're right—you and I will go."

[The director was a flagrant womanizer whose management style was to make smiling, slick efforts to psychologically coerce what he could simply ask for. Showing up for work most days around eleven was not an effective leadership strategy. His misogyny-laced humor was lame and crude.]

Later that week, we went out to Wilbur's little cement block efficiency cabin, and yes, that lunatic owned that poor, defeated woman, but there was nothing tangible and legal—not a fucking thing we could do.

We drove back to the office in silence. I could tell the director's guts were churning and for the first time in a couple of years, I liked him.

I understand that sexual abuse generally has to do more with power and a need to exert dominance than with sexual desire. One doesn't have to look very hard to see that, but I have to confess that I don't understand it. I am especially baffled by the seemingly commonplace linkage of power and dominance to sex. That's psychological terra incognita to me—incomprehensible on both sides of that equation.

I have never liked having power over other people.

[I was willing to do it for pay.]

I'm capable of being dominating and physically intimidating in a situation of necessity, but afterward I feel exhausted and depressed.

[Overall, I would prefer dental work.]

That ability has mainly been deployed against fellow males. Most of them were drunk.

[There was a period of time in my life when I left a trail of emotionally wounded women in my wake, but it wasn't due to the commonplace dysfunction(s) of male dominance—I was a different kind of asshole.]

Sex has always been a refuge from power and dominance for me, a place to safely relax into vulnerability, a haven from aggression, not a permission to engage in aggression. While I would love to claim this as a virtue, I can't because virtues are voluntary and this isn't. It's just the way I am. I don't know where that places me in the spectrum of male character.

[Guys don't talk much about such things.]

Many of the various behaviors that seem arguably "harmless" to the naïve, but clearly exist on the arc of the behavioral spectrum that ends in rape are charged with a hidden undercurrent of primal threat and their cumulative effect is a pervasive atmosphere of silent intimidation. Those of us who earnestly try not to contribute to the fear and intimidation have to realize that the dysfunctions of patriarchy have set the terms by which our actions and interactions are interpreted. Our culture has failed us, and men should be at least as pissed off as the women who are finally speaking out and being heard.

Have you ever hiked in a place of dense cover and plentiful rattlesnakes? I have and I can tell you that small, innocuous motions—a bird hopping from one low branch to another, a chipmunk ducking into a hole—trigger tiny jolts of alarm that pass so quickly most escape conscious attention. Though you tire a little more quickly than you would otherwise, sometimes you like it—that cranked up awareness gobbling every nuance and detail from the senses can be alluringly vibrant. But when you return to your home or campsite, or even the open space of a trail, your whole body sighs with subtle, delicious relief. What if you felt that hyper-alertness at home, on the street, at work, every time you went to the supermarket—in more places in your life than not? Think about those little trickles of adrenaline, those vague whiffs of fight-flight tension continually streaming through your daily life.

[And by the way, don't talk about it. You have a good life and no right to complain. Hell, it's your own fault anyway—those clothes, that makeup.]

What kinds of twists, kinks, and rages might that carve into your psyche?

[You don't have to physically harm someone to ruin his or her day or week or year.]

I find the apparently commonplace (among males) shutting down of empathy in sexual situations incomprehensible—mine opens wide and I admit that can be risky, but without it so much would probably seem dead and strange. It's a moot point because I can't control it—I open up—that's just how it works for me. So, one of my problems in attempting to write about this is that men are doing shit that I cannot sensibly imagine.

[The idea of wanting to grab a stranger's ass, genitals, or breast seems simply and self-evidently deranged.]

But violent abuse and rape are merely the far end of the spectrum of male dominant behavior in patriarchal culture. It's not difficult to backtrack along that spectrum until you find your own behavior (especially with help from women who are forsaking their silence) and when you do, you find yourself face to face with a moral imperative.

[I'm not necessarily a nonviolent guy—I try to be and I've gotten pretty good at it, but some of my early programming was really fucking gnarly. There are women dear to me who have been raped, and I have seen their scars up close. If you gave me a time machine, I would load my shotgun and hop in.]

This is a lot bigger than guys who are already basically kind and decent learning to show a bit more empathy. This is a major rewrite of rules that have been so thoroughly woven into the fabric of our culture that they've been functionally invisible and have had us all by the balls.

Deeply rooted (both ancient and modern) aspects of our culture will have to be dismantled. They should have been torn down long ago and now the need is urgent. We cannot just hand this off to evolution—we have to slide over into the driver's seat and steer.

Bea's father, Howard, came to our town in search of greener pastures and ostensibly to rebuild his relationship with the daughter he had largely abandoned many years before, in what I vaguely understood as an extended plunge into the depths of alcohol following the death of Bea's mother. Bea didn't offer many details, and I didn't seek them.

[I don't know if I refrained from questions out of kindness or self-absorption —probably a bit of both. Whatever direct or indirect permission was needed to open her history, I certainly failed to give it.]

Howard was a skilled machinist and had no problem finding work. He was capable of charm and seemed truly intent on a new start with his life. Though the notion that an alcoholic can simply reinvent himself as a nonalcoholic by moving to a new town was transparently absurd, his sober charm was sufficiently polished to win a period of grace, until he hopped off the wagon again.

One evening after a typically stressful day as a welfare caseworker, I arrived at Bea's apartment to find her being viciously berated by her very intoxicated father. My instant reaction was distinctly undiplomatic.

[I have a childhood history that rendered me reflexively and savagely intolerant of belligerent drunks.]

I said, "I think you should shut your fucking mouth or I'll have to throw your sorry ass out of here."

"Who do think you are talking to me like that?"

"It doesn't matter who I think I am. What matters is what you can do about it."

"I guess I'll have to think about that."

"Do it some place else. Get the fuck out of here."

He left.

Bea and I made love on the kitchen floor.

[Our love was doomed.]

The road to a new social environment will be (unavoidably) paved with misunderstandings, misdirected anger, confusion, ambiguity, and sometimes injustice.

[Fasten your seatbelts; it's going to be a hell of a ride.]

One of the problems we face as patriarchal culture implodes is that it's relatively easy to incorporate arbitrary rules into a social structure, but what we have to do now is replace formulae with fluidity. There are no guidelines for that.

[You might call this cultural democracy.]

When we met, my wife was seventeen, and I was twenty-six. She was married. I was her caseworker. Our affair that took nearly four years to become a marriage began a little more than a year later (after I was no longer her caseworker) with an eagerly welcomed, impulsive kiss. One of the best, wisest things I ever did was to propose to a married woman in the shower.

[If human beings meeting in the confluence of love and desire are required to deny the delicious anarchy of the human heart, life will hose them hard. The alternative is to recognize the heroism of gentleness and embrace its risks.]

The conventionally religious tend to find great comfort in hierarchies and in codified restraints in speech and behavior supported by divine edict, despite complications like chronic guilt, war, and sexual frustration—it gives them a sense of order and meaning. When they encounter progressive ideas, they over-react (communism! perversion! the end times!) as if their very world is threatened. No one should be surprised by this.

[When you are knocked to the floor and kicked by your ranting, cursing father, it rearranges the molecular structure of your spirit.]

If a woman from my past spoke up about feeling threatened or intimidated, I would apologize—not as a tacit admission of conscious wrongdoing, but because I was part of a situation that caused discomfort. "I'm sorry," is simply Civility 101. It is not noble, conciliatory, or politically correct. It is polite.

I find the more mundane and commonplace sins relatively easy to imagine. I can imaginatively put myself into the mindset of someone desperate enough to steal, fearful or embarrassed enough to lie, so enthralled with an attraction as to have a hidden affair, angry enough in a moment to lash out shamefully. But to me, rape is getting over into Jeffrey Dahmer territory—the realm of the unimaginable. I can't enter into the mindset of someone who keeps human body parts in their refrigerator and I can't imagine the urge to rape.

[It baffles me.]

I once taught an evening class in painting as an adjunct at a community college, mostly for the experience and because teaching was enormously satisfying, even after the inescapable loads of peripheral horseshit were factored in.

Around mid-semester, one of my nontraditional students asked to speak to me in private. The local police had gone to an apartment to arrest a man on a parole violation. He fled and was arrested after a high-speed chase. In the trunk of his car they found an extensive file of photographs of the student taken surreptitiously using a telephoto lens over a period of several months. To the best of her knowledge, she had never met the man. Even though he was in jail and likely would be for a while, she couldn't be certain he had been working alone, and anyway, her sense of safety and security in the world had been shattered. I made sure that either I or a trustworthy fellow student escorted her to her car after each class for the balance of the semester.

[How many years did it take for her fear to subside?]

My father was both a fierce protector and a batterer. In his presence, I was safe from everything but his wrath and ridicule.

[Beloved animals met terrible fates in the confluence of paternal PTSD and maternal sociopathy.]

I carry parts of my father that are both admirable and poignantly defective. I have protective instincts that have served me well at times, but also tend to override other useful things like logic, reason, and civilized behavior. When someone I feel intuitively connected to suffers sudden misfortune, it feels to variable degrees like it's my fault—as if I have failed somehow. It wasn't something I did, rather something I didn't do.

[That's the narrow defile in which chronic depression ambushes me. I know this and my ability to articulate it in both words and images lends a clarity that enables me to largely refuse the anger that bubbles up from the ground of my childhood.]

I don't think that kind of guilt is at all unusual among American, especially Appalachian, males. So when a torrent of *"me too"* stories washes over them sparking and crackling with cognitive dissonance, failure, and fear, a sensible, considered, at least partially honest response has a likelihood comparable to winning lottery tickets.

Over the course of twenty-one years (with a few wandering interludes) I was first a caseworker and then a casework supervisor for the Pennsylvania Department of Public Welfare. I had made referrals that resulted in children being removed from households and placed in foster care due to abuse milder than what I had endured as a child, but I had never identified myself as having been an abused child. I have neither a neat clinical nor an insightfully poetic explanation for that. My observation from experience is that trauma often works that way.

After I finished my Master of Arts degree at age forty, my bother, Denny said he wanted to take me on a fishing trip as a graduation present. We drove to Pulaski, New York, checked into a motel, and met our guide before dawn the following morning over a high-cholesterol breakfast at a local diner.

We spent most of the day floating the Salmon River in a dory-like aluminum boat. The guide gave us advice on where to cast our surface plugs and controlled the action of the lures in the current by back paddling with the oars. The conversation was mostly light-hearted banter spiced with gentle irony and mellowed by a love of the river.

Ospreys and kingfishers worked the river ahead of us, in their own way. Soothed by sun, breeze, water, and birdsong into the mellow relaxation of work and indolence, we were alert and idle, as the well-fed wild should be. A day that began long ended short.

We drove into the highway night keenly feeling our brotherhood, the shared blood and history we had too long busily neglected. After lapsing briefly into the hypnotic rhythm of the road, Denny spoke.

"I had an ulterior motive when I invited you on this trip."

"Yeah, I had that feeling."

"We need to talk about what went on when we were growing up."

"It was pretty crazy."

"No, it was worse than that."

We talked each other through the dark realities of our father's rage, our mother's dishonesty and manipulation, and the shared violence our parents unleashed on our bodies, our selves, our lives, and our abilities to love, feel, and trust. He told me, with a frankness rendered bearable by darkness and driving, of his own struggle with crippled self-esteem, insidiously persistent fear of betrayal, and depression that had wrestled him to the brink of psychological disaster. The strength of his wife, his love, and his inner self had pulled him back from that terrible edge, and he realized that I too, had either been there or would surely find myself there in the future.

"Get counseling," he said. "You can't deal with this on your own and you *will* have to deal with this. Find a counselor you can connect with. Give it a chance, but if you don't feel a genuine rapport after three or four sessions, try someone else. But don't give up. Work it all the way out."

He saved my life.

[And now, men and women must save each other with the truth of their stories.]

Jake

Jake was manic, delusional, and often drunk. He wore a surplus army trench coat buttoned tightly around his neck, all year round. The bottle of cheap muscatel he usually had in one of the coat's voluminous pockets looked and smelled like kerosene. He would take a hit off the bottle during the interview, offer me some, and act seriously insulted when I refused. He would rant and babble so relentlessly about whatever was rippling through his addled brain that it was impossible to keep an interview on track.

His manic energy radiated potential violence.

I was alone in our Philipsburg outpost office when Jake came in, sat down in front of my desk, and said, "Mr. Darling, I want to get my nuts cut off."

"Why is that, Jake?"

"Don't want nothing to do with women no more and I figure if I get my nuts cut off all that energy will go into strength, just like a young pig."

"Did you talk to your doctor about that?"

"Yeah, he wouldn't do it. You know what I think? I think he's a goddamned Catholic!"

"Has anything changed in your situation that you need to tell me about?"

"I threw my wife out."

"Any chance you'll get back together?"

"No! Never. I caught her in bed with my best friend's wife. I should never have married her. I met her in a whorehouse in Washington, D.C. She fucked rich niggers for seven hundred dollars an hour and gave it all up for me."

"I have to ask you to go down to domestic relations at the court house."

"I already went there. I told them I wanted to shoot the goddamned, lezzie sumbitch, and you know what they told me?"

"What?"

"They told me it was illegal to shoot a goddamned, lezzie sumbitch!"

"I think they're right, Jake, and you don't need any more trouble with the law right now."

"Here, have a drink."

"You know I can't drink on the job."

"I want to get my nuts cut off."

I really wanted him to go away. His speech was getting more and more agitated. He was sweating profusely and taking big gulps of wine. So, I gave him a brochure from family planning and said, "These are the people you should talk to about that."

"I'm going down there right now."

"That's a good idea, Jake. I'll recalculate your food stamps and send you a notice."

An hour later the phone rang. It was family planning. An angry voice said, "Don't ever do that to me again."

I said, "You, of all people, should understand just how desperate I was."

[A moment of silence followed by a loud click.]

Between a Rock and a Soft Place

(for Lehman "Dar" Dowdy, 1938–2011)

After a Maine coast epiphany on my first real vacation in far too long, I returned home to northwestern Pennsylvania determined to mend my workaholic ways. I needed to open more space and time in my life for a long list of satisfactions great and small and for my son, Oren, who had lately ascended to a new level in his blossoming abilities. It was time for our shared adventures to become more complex and vigorous. I wanted to encourage Oren to wander in both the library and the forest and unite those two realms with imagination, intellect, and hiking boots by engaging in a quest.

I had recently read a locally published book about Cornplanter, the chief who had guided the Seneca Nation of Indians through the tumult of white settlement and the American Revolution. Though aspects of the book were of doubtful veracity, its story of Cornplanter's Cave was corroborated by several other sources. The legend is that as a young man, Cornplanter tracked a wounded deer to its final refuge in the mouth of a cave. When he explored the cave, he found a long narrow passageway leading to a large room with a pool of water harboring blind fish. On the walls of the chamber there were pictographs left by the Erie Indians who had been displaced from what became Seneca territory long ago in a war so brutal that its collective guilt left permanent scars on the tribal psyche. For the rest of his life, Cornplanter went to the cave to meditate when faced with difficult decisions. A claimed rediscovery of the cave in the 1940s was almost certainly false, but in the 1880s a white man wrote about finding and entering the cave and didn't appear to have regarded his discovery as extraordinary—it was simply part of the story of his time in the Alleghenies. With regard to the cave, he had neither axe nor ego to grind. His account gave the most geographically explicit description of the cave's location, but it was still pretty vague.

[One can't rule out the possibility that his description of the location was deliberately misleading.]

Tracy Ridge, in the heart of ancient Seneca territory, became the starting point for a spring and summer of long wandering hikes in search of that Holy Grail. A well-known hiking trail traversed the area, and we mostly stayed away from it on the assumption that anything to be found in the immediate vicinity of the trail would have been found by others long ago.

As longtime lovers of the sandstone conglomerate rock formations of the Allegheny Plateau (despite the occasional presence of rattlesnakes), we were well aware of the shapes indicated on topographical maps that signaled the likely presence of outcroppings and hence caves. But we also kept our agendas open to impulsive roaming, hunches, unrelated distractions, and the possibility that the cave might be found in an unexpected place.

Purpose, history, and mystery provided the incentive to Oren's young mind that the need for the forest's quiet beauty provided for my middle-aged recovering workaholic mind. I had no objective expectation of finding the cave and thought that, even if it really did exist, its entrance may have been naturally or deliberately obliterated long ago. Still, our quest was more than merely a fatherly ruse—Cornplanter's cave had just enough of a faint aura of real possibility to add a note of shared excitement to our meandering hikes.

As the summer passed and our half purposeful and half random searches filled the map, we paused to consider the blank spaces. Though most people seem to prefer the organized, synthetic cues of trails to the seeming chaos of wild forest, human senses snag on features both subtle and obvious and steer wandering in particular ways even without trails. When people wander, they tend to wander the same ways. The feet of a large enough number of roaming people would likely create trails even without practical or recreational destinations. I realized that if we wanted to find something unseen by generations of wanderers, we had to get methodical in resisting the natural drift of our attention.

[Cornplanter himself didn't find the cave in territory known intimately by his people for generations by following known routes or by wandering. He found

the cave when the practical necessity of tracking disengaged him from normal
pathways of trails, experience, and attention.]

When we studied our topographical maps and penciled in rough remembrances of our hikes, we discovered that we had misidentified a small creek, and as a result, one of several blank spots in the pattern of our search was in the area I thought most likely to be the site of the cave. Our hikes had flowed around the most promising possibility as water flows around a rock in a stream. It was elusive—finding it required conscious resistance to the subliminal promptings of the land. We had to use and trust the map.

The area of open, grassy forest scattered with kitchen appliance-sized boulders had special resonance. It was a place of ease and comfort. The first time we traversed the area we saw nothing notable beyond the pastoral gentleness of its beauty. But being freshly attuned to the way our search was subliminally steered by features on the peripheries of attention, I realized that we were probably still flowing around the rock in the stream. When we returned, I had a feeling—a deer hunter's intuition that has brought me far more meat than luck can logically claim. We sat a while and then searched as if for the lost blood trail of a wounded deer.

We paused often as we walked a meandering spiral out from the center of the area. A great slab of rock, a polygon eighteen inches thick, eight feet tall, and eight feet wide, stood, strikingly visible yet inexplicably difficult to notice, plumb vertical on gently sloping ground. It seemed self-evidently not a natural formation.

[This was an admittedly non-expert impression, but every natural scenario I could conjure was neatly sliced in half by Occam's Razor.]

Our sense of questing, of searching evaporated as we sat next to the rock. We felt as though we had found whatever was to be found. When we began our quest, we had agreed that if we discovered the cave, we would tell no one, unless we found someone trustworthy from the Seneca Nation. We felt the same way about the monolith. It seemed sacred. I took a close, trusted friend there to confirm our impressions, which he did.

I returned to the monolith several times over the following few years, both with and without Oren. Every time I went there, I had to find it by resisting the subliminal promptings of the landscape to enter its area and then by searching as if trying to pick up the lost blood trail of a wounded deer. I have a very good sense of direction—all my life I've been able to feel the cardinal directions as naturally as right and left. I can feel the shape of the land beneath my feet and use that knowledge to navigate. In years of bushwhack wandering in the Alleghenies, my compass remained in the little emergency kit stowed in the bottom of my daypack. I had never before experienced such difficulty in finding my way back to a known place.

I felt a palpable sacredness much like what I had felt in a handful of other special forest places, but here it was sharper, less diffuse because it had a perceptible epicenter—the monolith. Though I'm wary of new age-ish naiveté and pretense, I don't know what to call it but energy.

[I realize these impressions are gigantically subjective.]

Oren and I shared a longstanding reverence for Native American culture and were keenly aware that we were walking in Cornplanter's home territory. I can't argue that we weren't predisposed to feeling a special spiritual charge in such a place and circumstance, but I carry a deeply ingrained skepticism along with my openness to mystery.

[Mystery embraced without rigorous skepticism too easily devolves into superstition.]

All my life, I have experienced places of concentrated sacredness where pausing quietly is akin to prayer and I know many others who feel it too. When I bring them to my places or they bring me to theirs, we nearly always agree. Such agreement hardly constitutes scientific or even journalistic objectivity, but I don't cling to this experience as something to be analyzed, defended, disputed, or even clearly defined. I hold it lightly in grateful acceptance. I have no need to make a belief of it.

The monolith stayed with me. It seemed important. Though the finding of it seemed freighted with unknown purpose that I couldn't explain, I was comfortable living with its mystery. I entrusted the way and time to tell of what we had found to fate.

[I don't really believe in fate, but it's a handy place to file future possibilities that have exhausted their potential for further thought and can only be revived by serendipity.]

A strange and difficult decade passed. A weird and unholy alliance of corporate industry and the United States Forest Service set upon the Allegheny Plateau like a starving dog and chewed it ragged. I retired from nearly thirty years in state government. Places of present love and ancestral rootedness were ravaged into gridworks of oil and gas wells, access roads, tank farms, and brine ponds. I dabbled in activism as much to quell the angry monkey wrench urges that erupted in my heart as for any real hope of successful resistance. On the local environmental front, the steady convergence of political realism and cynicism was a ghastly replay of the early seventies protest movement. I needed something more true and satisfying than the weary token efforts of meetings, letters, and handing out leaflets. So did my friend, Cathy Pedler, a dedicated fulltime environmental activist; and for her, that other something was volunteering at the Faithkeepers School on the Seneca Nation of Indians reservation. Cathy and her husband, Dave, were both archeologists, and through their fieldwork, they had become friends with Dar and Sandy Dowdy who had founded the charter school to ensure that the Seneca language, culture, and spirituality would continue to be passed on to new generations. Cathy invited me to come to the school and meet Dar, Sandy, and the kids, and I became part of the program without engaging in anything that a career bureaucrat like me would have called a decision-making process. Dar and Sandy were very articulate, but they were also very much at ease with shared understanding communicated by nuances of intonation and body language. Dar spoke of that understanding as speaking from the heart, rather than the mind.

Cathy's and my job was to teach a group of children ranging from mid-grade school to mid-teens to be at ease in the woods, to reconnect them to wild land as a place of beauty, comfort, and abundance. I scouted out some nearby areas and found two small creek valleys that had everything we needed: a variety of vegetation ranging from meadow to mature second growth forest, game trails, animal tracks, edible plants, wildflowers, and topography amenable to basic lessons in navigation. The Faithkeepers School woods outing became a weekly event.

Dar's physical activities were limited by congestive heart failure, so he didn't join us on the outings (Sandy nearly always did), but most days he was hanging out on the school's front porch or on the grounds when we returned from the woods. Our conversations began and rambled in ways that would look idle to nonnative Americans. But from vague beginnings, stories flowed in both directions. Dar told me that the preservation and revival of Seneca culture at this point in history was in keeping with the teaching and prophecies of Handsome Lake, the great Seneca/Iroquois spiritual leader (1735–1815) and half brother of Cornplanter. Handsome Lake had prophesied the tragic and ruthless theft of the Seneca's homeland to build the Kinzua Dam on the Allegheny River.

The bulk of Handsome Lake's teachings have been transmitted orally. As a matter of intuitive courtesy, I only asked direct questions about the Longhouse Religion to clarify something that had been volunteered. I left it up to Dar to decide what was appropriate to tell the white-guy volunteer. In retrospect, I have sometimes thought that I may have been too shy in that respect, but it seemed appropriate to err on the side of gentleness and trust.

Dar told me that the fiftieth anniversary of the building of the Kinzua Dam and the removal of the Senecas from their land would be the beginning of a new cycle of Handsome Lake's prophecies. Certain ceremonies were to be performed in preparation. A messenger would come to them to tell where the ceremonies should be held.

[Dar told me much more, both directly and by implication, but that is a Seneca story to tell, not mine.]

One day, when Dar thanked me for what I was doing with the children, I replied that it was truly my pleasure and told him how I missed the times I had spent in the woods with my son when he was growing up and about our quest for the Holy Grail of Cornplanter's Cave. Dar said, "We're not so interested in Cornplanter. Cornplanter was mean—he had to be—that's not the spirit we want to teach here. It was Handsome Lake who brought us wisdom and peace."

A couple weeks later, Dar told me that when the Seneca's were forcibly removed from their land, they asked for a delay so the elder women could complete a cycle of teaching the younger ones about medicinal plants. The delay wasn't granted and a great deal of knowledge was lost in the subsequent disruption. I told Dar that when I was a child some Seneca people used to set up a stand on Liberty Street in downtown Warren on Saturday mornings. My mother bought sassafras root bark from them, and I was very fond of the strong dark tea she made from it. Dar said, "That was my mother—she sold herbs there. I used to help her out." We both smiled at the notion that we had probably met long ago.

Dar said, "Where is that rock you told me about?"

I described the location as clearly as I could.

"That's interesting."

Not long after that, the Allegheny Defense Project held a gathering not far from the beginning of my hiking route to the monolith so, while attending the gathering, I hiked (alone) to the rock and shot a roll of thirty-five millimeter film of it from every angle. At the gathering, when Cathy said she would be seeing Dar and Sandy the next day, I handed her the roll of film and said, "Give this to Dar." When the film was processed, the photographs all showed lights seeming to dance in the air around the rock. I assumed this was some sort of anomaly in the processing, but Dar believed that the lights had meaning. He had seen this kind of thing before.

After my next outing with the kids from the school, Dar and I had another rambling conversation. He told me about seeing an eagle the previous week and that he felt the eagle was telling him something; it was a messenger. Then he said, "Would you be willing to talk to some folks about that rock?"

"Sure—as long as it's not the Forest Service."

Dar laughed and said, "No, it won't be the Forest Service, just some Seneca people. We'll set something up."

Sandy e-mailed me a few days later with a meeting time. I was expecting a few old friends of Dar's, but the conference room's circle of chairs was filled. I told the whole story of searching for the cave, finding the rock, my intuitions about it, and my reluctance to reveal its location to anyone but the Seneca people. There was talk about a similar stone found in the vicinity of Oil City, eighty miles south and a group of much smaller ones on the portion of the original land grant that remained above water, but the conversation mostly flowed around the topic like creek water around a stone. Dar asked if I would take Sandy and some others from the school to see the monolith and I said, "Of course." I would have done that as a matter of friendship, but I had been drawn into a realization that this was something important at such a gentle and natural pace that my giving involved no sense of obligation and caused no debt.

I made three more trips. The first was with Sandy and a group of teachers and students from the school, the second with a few teenage students and two people from the Seneca Nation Conservation Department, who recorded the exact location of the site on their GPS and marked a boat landing site at the nearest access via the Allegheny Reservoir. The third was with Dave and Cathy, whose archeological expertise confirmed my impression that the monolith was indeed an artifact and not merely a geological anomaly.

I felt an unexpected sense of relief, as though a great but invisible burden had been lifted from my shoulders. When I told Dar this, he smiled and said, "Yeah, you had to carry that message a long time."

Meanwhile, Dar's congestive heart failure had been following its inevitable course and an oxygen tank became his constant companion. The Seneca Nation Conservation Department outfitted a wheelchair with extensions so it could be carried by a strong foursome and modified a boat to accommodate the wheelchair. Dar was partly floated, partly carried, and partly wheeled to the monolith, where ceremonies were conducted.

[Was I the messenger Dar told me about? It certainly seems that I was a messenger of some sort, but I don't like the way my ego rises to that bait.]

Shortly after that, I received a package in the mail from an old friend and avid birder. In the package were several large feathers. One was labeled "brown pelican"—she knew of my fondness for pelicans—and another was labeled "bald eagle." She told me she had sent the eagle feather because it felt borrowed —it didn't truly belong to her. Being given an eagle feather by a fellow Buddhist was the most flattering felony I have ever indulged, but it didn't feel like it belonged to me either. I decided I should give it to Dar, but my perennial busyness (writing, painting, wandering, and some medical issues of my own) stretched days into weeks. Then Cathy called to tell me that Dar had passed away.

I took the eagle feather to the monolith. The witch hazel growing next to the rock was adorned with small bundles of tobacco from the Seneca ceremonies, and I fastened the eagle feather there with a deerskin lace. Once again, though in a smaller way, I felt unburdened.

[I don't know what it all means. Perhaps the lesson herein for me is about doing the right thing without the assurance of knowing the real meaning. Believing in that possibility requires great faith in the fundamental goodness of the world—a faith not easily given. We all need a little help. I was both delivering and receiving a message. Perhaps that's our perpetual condition, or perhaps it should be.]

The Seneca Nation flag Dar gave me hangs in Oren's apartment.

Pronoun Dysphoria

[I feel as though I should begin nearly every paragraph with a series of disclaimers. I hate when that happens.]

Language is powerful. We all know its capacity to render accurate description, express our many levels and layers of emotion and perception, to give pleasure, and to deceive.

[Language's power to wound, dominate, and punish is what renders things like racial epithets so abhorrent.]

All languages have built-in biases that can either lead discourse astray or create blind spots that obscure, rather than reveal, truths. The more fundamental the truths thus obscured the more insidious the effect and when the dysfunction is rooted in grammar itself, rather than merely in n-words and f-words and slang usages of words that might otherwise be innocent, the resulting distortions can be socially established as unspoken and therefore unexamined truths.

[I realize that, in two short paragraphs, I've laid out a subject that could easily occupy a large book that I have neither the desire nor the discipline to write.]

A great deal of interesting and much needed discussion about the way gender biases are subtly and sometimes not so subtly encoded in language and grammar is rippling through the world nowadays. I don't have any particularly astute or unique observations to add to that conversation.

The dominant "he" is not the small thing it's easy to wish it were, and as a writer, I long for a simple, graceful way to subvert the deference to male identity

English insidiously imposes on our narratives. It's tempting to advocate the invention of new set of genderless pronouns (perhaps we could appropriate them from Farsi), but frankly that would be an awkward pain-in-the-ass for at least a generation, if not longer, and meanwhile, I would prefer not have readers stumble and stutter over my sentences anymore than necessary. I already cause enough of that by accident.

I don't have a solution to propose or the means to implement it, if I did. Language changes by evolution, not by decree.

[Encountering "he/she" in mid sentence amidst otherwise graceful prose is like tripping on a crack in the sidewalk. Perhaps, it's better to switch it up at random and let context take care of the rest, thus encouraging he and she to evolve toward neutrality.]

But there's another problem with pronouns and it's easier to address without becoming unintelligible, awkward, or silly-assed correct. It's important and maybe it could lead the way in evolving other reforms. Ironically, my personal solution involves the use of gender-based pronouns because for now, like it or not, they're all we've got.

The grammatically correct pronoun for an animal is "it." An animal is never a "who," but always a "that." This is absurd and fundamentally false, a grammatical dysfunction that gives tacit permission to immense cruelties.

[I am not a vegetarian. Sometimes I eat animals and sometimes I kill them myself. Nevertheless, I believe that, as sentient beings, animals do, indeed, have rights.

Many of the individual animals and animal species I love eat other animals. It's strange, scary, and poignant, but so too are earthquakes, parasites, house fires, and Trump supporters.]

Language that classifies things like cats and moose in the same category as hammers and beer cans is stupidly crude and blunt.

[If you don't understand the difference between a hammer and a mammal, see your doctor. The right combination of medication and counseling may help.]

In my own writing, I've adopted a fairly simple alternative—when I know the gender of the animal, I refer to them using the appropriate gender specific pronoun. If I don't know the gender, I use my own because I think that, when in doubt, it is best to err on the side of identifying with the creature whose story is being told, to not omit the animal's sentience from the story.

[My cat, Milo is not a thing, an object, or an it. Milo is a male sentient being, a he.]

The very simple, ancient knowledge that, in relation to other living creatures, we have more common ground than difference needs to be rewoven into the fabric of language as a simple matter of descriptive accuracy. Truth is incomplete without it.

Will, Bill, and Rupert

Part One

Though William Gifford Deshner died in 1943, six years before I was born, his charismatic presence echoed through our family's stories so vividly that he seemed as tangibly active in my childhood world as a living person. He was my great-grandfather. His daughter, Wilda, and her husband, Rollin David Wilson (aka Baldy) were my mother's parents.

The stories told about Will Deshner were abundant, earthy, ordinary, and reverent. He was a skilled carpenter, worked extraordinarily hard, and was loved equally by the pious and wild branches of the family. He was devotedly active in his community's Free Methodist church, but he also enjoyed sampling Baldy's prohibition-era homebrew. He took long solitary walks in the woods, sometimes even in thunderstorms. He had a grade school education. The family stories mostly centered around his distinctive blend of humor and wisdom—like the time he told his grandson, Bill, when they were shingling the roof on a tall building, "If you drop your hammer, make sure you let go of it."

I first encountered Will Deshner's journal in 1968. Aunt Gert (Will Deshner's eldest grandchild) and her husband, Ed, had moved back to Mayburg, Pennsylvania, the long defunct village of their birth and youth, after maintaining one of the remaining original houses there as a camp and family gathering place for many years. I was a student at Clarion State College (now Clarion

University) fifty miles away. This was a strange and difficult time in my life, during which I often sought respite and healing in the familiar woods of my youth and ancestors. Gert and Ed offered an always available refuge in the form of a spare room, a seat at the dinner table, and a back door that opened onto miles of loved and familiar forest. On one of my weekend visits, Gert showed me a volume of my great-grandfather's journal. I was immediately interested because I had recently begun keeping a journal of my own, and Will Deshner's recurring mentions of my favorite forest places bespoke a kinship deeper than mere ancestry.

Volumes of the journal circulated among my mother's siblings, and I was always eager for an opportunity to peruse one, but it wasn't until many years later that I was able to borrow a volume from Gert's daughter, Judy, and read it from beginning to end. In it, I found more questions than answers, more mystery than knowledge and I became hungry for more. Meanwhile, Uncle Dick (Richard Wilson) had gathered all the other known volumes because he believed they should be kept together.

Dick and I weren't close when I was growing up, but as an adult, I felt an easy natural rapport with him, and the e-mail dialogue (Dick had moved to Florida in retirement.) that arose from my questions about the journal often rambled in other directions. After several years of correspondence, Dick gave me all the journal volumes in his possession. He said trusted me to do the right thing with them.

[One volume is missing in action.]

The journal consists of one line per day, written across both open pages of hardbound ledgers, from 1903 to 1942. In the beginning, it was only a record of work done and pay received, but Will Deshner gradually began adding information about weather and events outside the realm of his work. In part, he may have begun noting other things so that a blank day wouldn't be misconstrued as an omission. The writing is very spare—events are stated, but not described. Though reading a few pages imparts an impression so mundane that one can't help wondering what could have motivated him to persist through thirty-nine years of daily practice, the days accumulating into thousands bespeak an intensity far beyond his meager words. As one reads onward, an image of the man and his life, faded and cracked like an old, yellowed photograph, emerges.

[I find great hope in the rising of that faded image.]

I had the journal transcribed and then, after a several year struggle with reformatting, proofing, my highly variable motivation, and the competing demands of my own writing, published it via print on demand so it would be available to anyone (especially family) who was interested.

The original now resides in the collection of the Warren County Historical Society.

[Like Dick, I hadn't taken ownership of the journal; I had taken responsibility for its fate.]

Part Two

Baldy had driven the train from Mayburg to Sheffield when he learned that Wilda was in labor with their second child. He decided to make the return trip, even though there was an ice jam in progress on the Tionesta Creek.

[The Tionesta Creek would be called a river anywhere else.]

He drove the locomotive as fast as he dared in the strange silver half-light of a New Year's full moon. The rising ice was closing over the tracks in the visible distance behind him as he raced down the creekside. Baldy and Wilda's eldest son was born that night. They named him William Deshner Wilson, after Wilda's father; they called him "Bill."

Uncle Bill became my primary source of clarification for the assorted gem-like mysteries I found scattered through my great grandfather's journal.

[I needed more than answered questions; I needed stories.]

Bill savored storytelling at a gentle, leisurely pace, and listening to his stories was a fine way to spend an afternoon.

Bill once said about his grandfather, "He wasn't just a good man—there are lots of those— he was a great man, and those are scarce."

Part Three

From Will Deshner's journal:

March 1929

17	S	O.E. Rupert was Drounded to Day	30 Clear 6	S
18	10	Reparing Generator on large engin	39 Clear 13	10
19	4	Reparing acid still Down to Kellittville hunting Rupert		4
20	10	Reparing crude acid column		10
21		hunting Rupert at Porter farm		
22	10	Reparing finishing column	Rain and warm	10
23	10	Reparing acid column		10
24	S	Down to bucksmills hunting Rupert		S

Bill told me the backstory: O.E. Rupert was a rarity in the waning timber boom of the Tionesta boondocks—a (relatively) cultured man. He lived with his brother in Truemans near the confluence of Fool's Creek and the Tionesta, a few miles upstream from Mayburg. He regularly crossed the creek on a swinging footbridge and followed the railroad grade downstream to Mayburg, where he gave music lessons in the homes of his pupils. The last lessons of the day were reserved for Mayburg's Italian enclave, where the residents bartered homemade beer and wine for his services. After one well-paid evening of violin lessons, he failed to negotiate the swinging bridge.

Part Four

Once, during my hippie wanderings of the early seventies, when I was broke and burdened by aching tenderness for a lost love, a friend repaid a small, forgotten loan from long before. I decided to put a large quantity of good food in my belly. I chose a particular restaurant partly because I was unlikely to encounter a familiar face there. I preferred not to be distracted from my fine blend of melancholy, existential anguish, and self-pity.

I ordered a ham steak because it was one of the biggest meals I could get with my meager windfall, and seeing it on the menu evoked memories from a younger, happier time, when I was camping with Uncle Bill, in the old Mayburg Park. We had fished all day and as we relaxed into mellow exhaustion, Bill put a ham steak on the grill. We ate with the natural gusto of well earned hunger, and Bill told hunting, fishing, Mayburg, and Baldy stories until the delicious fatigue that comes after a long day well spent outdoors overtook us. It was one of the most idyllic, contented evenings of my life.

The memory lifted me. I basked in the remembered warmth of fishing, sunshine, and campfire and as I settled into the sensual pleasures of eating, my funk dissipated like morning fog on a sunny day.

Many years later, I told Bill that story. He grinned and said, "That's the way it's supposed to work, isn't it."

Part Five

In the spring of 2012, Bill was hospitalized after injuring his shoulder in a fall.

While I was visiting him, a social worker came to explain to Bill that he would have to be transferred to a nursing home for an indefinite period of "transitional care" with the goal of enabling him to return home to Sheffield and his nearly blind wife.

[Bill had a large and understandable, if only partially rational, loathing for nursing homes—at age ninety-one he had seen too many loved ones vanish into them never to be seen again. The nursing home they wanted to send him to was the same one Gert had died in the previous year.]

The social worker's body language was radiant with dissonance. The "goal" was a motivational ploy i.e. bullshit. Bill knew it. I knew it. He didn't say that he knew it, and I went along with it, because if I cooked up a ruse, spirited him out of there, and took him to Bobbs Creek (his favorite trout stream) to die, I would get in serious trouble of several kinds.

[There was something hard as flint in Bill's eyes.]

After the social worker left, Bill tried to get out of bed. I talked him out of it and distracted him with questions about Will Deshner's journal. Remembrance raised his spirits. He said there was a story he had intended to tell me since I had asked him about O.E. Rupert's drowning, but had forgotten on earlier occasions.

One summer, when the circus came to Sheffield, two elephants escaped during the night. They found their way to the Tionesta Creek and followed it. Meanwhile, the Rupert brothers had been on a serious bender. They awoke one morning befogged and befuddled by the hangover haze of moonshine, staggered out onto their porch overlooking the Tionesta Creek, and saw elephants frolicking in the water in joyful freedom. They summoned their neighbors to ask them if the spectacle was real.

Then he tried to get out of bed again. I asked him if he needed more pain medication and he said, "Yes." The busy nurses didn't respond to the buzzer. Bill started fumbling with his I.V. as if trying to figure out how to unhook it. I put my hands on his shoulders, looked into his eyes, and said, "Bill, if you fall now, you're going to be in a world of shit, and I'm going to feel like it was my fault. Please don't do this to me. I'll go get a nurse and get you some more pain medication, but you have to promise me you won't get out of bed while I do that."

He looked away.

"Bill, look at me."

Our eyes met.

"Do you promise you won't get out of bed while I get the nurse?"

"Okay."

Bill kept his promise. The nurse apologetically admitted Bill was long overdue for his pain medication and helped him move into a more comfortable position on the bed. The tension in his voice and eyes ebbed with the quickness of intravenous morphine, but so too did a visible measure of the gentle, but acute alertness that defined so much of Bill.

Assuming that Bill would tire easily, I had intended my visit to be brief, but now I was afraid that as soon as I left, he would try to get out of bed again, and the distraction of my company seemed comforting. Judy arrived as Bill's lunch was brought in and she assisted him with her perfect, inimitable blend of authority and kindness. Shortly after lunch, a volunteer from hospice came to sit with Bill. We said our goodbyes, and I promised to visit again the next day.

A few hours later, Bill was transported to the nursing home by ambulance and died while his daughter, Linda, was completing the admission papers. He made his getaway, after all.

At Bill's funeral in Sheffield, a group of local veterans performed a military ceremony with such stilted awkwardness that it was embarrassing and pathetic, even though their reverence was real and touching. The twenty-one-gun salute outside seemed harshly inappropriate for a man of Bill's extraordinary gentleness.

[Bill served in the Navy during World War Two and saw heavy action in the South Pacific. He never talked about it.]

Then the preacher quoted scriptures until I was ready to drop to my knees and beg for mercy. His hour of alternations between scriptural passages and prayers was wearisome in ways he was incapable of perceiving. He was relatively young and innocently kind, but he seemed smarter than his words, and that was weirdly poignant in a situation that already had a surplus of poignancy.

[A seven-inch brook trout is the greatest miracle one should ever need.]

I began to rant in my head about the way the minister's professed humility veiled an arrogance utterly at odds with Bill's spirit, but then I remembered that so too was my irritation and impatience.

[If you drop your hammer, make sure you let go of it.]

Part Six

I drove to Mayburg, intending to hike one of the routes I had gleaned from Will Deshner's journal. Though I had roamed the surrounding Allegheny National Forest for decades, I hadn't visited Mayburg itself in several years. I parked my truck at Gert and Ed's former residence, now a camp owned by their grandson. On the way in, I saw that all the old, communal shortcuts had been closed off with gates and "No Trespassing" signs— the walking route to the long abandoned railroad grade that follows the Tionesta Creek was easily twice its former distance.

[Times had changed and little trickles of urban toxicity had leaked into the boondocks.]

I set out on my own alternative route through the woods intending to cross Kingsley Run, a small tributary of the Tionesta, a short distance upstream from Mayburg, traverse the ridge to the east into the lower end of Frozen Eddy Run, and pick up on my originally intended route at Frozen Eddy's confluence with the Tionesta. Once again, my route was blocked by posted property lines, so I had to hike much farther upstream to the remains of the old dam that once held Mayburg's water supply. The inconvenience was well compensated. Though the dam hadn't held water in my lifetime, it still held a flood of memories—fishing alone and with Gert and my grandfather, a stoned sunlit afternoon making love with my first true love, a summer of 1969 marijuana patch eaten by deer. Sunlight, birdsong, and cobalt sky gently, but firmly, pulled me back into the here and now.

I climbed the ridge, crossed over into the headwaters of Frozen Eddy, climbed again to the ridgetop between Frozen Eddy and Phelps Run, and followed it northward to a clearing that yields a broad, breathtaking view of the Tionesta Valley.

[Frozen Eddy Run and Phelps Run are the first and second Tionesta Creek tributaries upstream from Mayburg.]

My original plan had evaporated—I was wandering now, letting the land lead me into its shapes and wonders.

[A pile of bear shit at the edge of the clearing, reminded me that wildness still lived there.]

The easiest descent into Phelps Run was an oblique angle back south and slightly east, to the headwaters, where the main branch breaks up into several small spring seeps. It's a beautiful, steep-sided little valley, and its spaciousness in early spring, before the trees fully leaf out, is so lovely that it's both lonely and joyous.

I followed the stream to its confluence with the Tionesta and followed the old railroad grade that parallels the creek back toward Mayburg. At the mouth of Frozen Eddy, I felt a fleeting urge to climb the ridge again and search for the beech tree bearing my great-grandfather's carved initials that I found the same year the deer ate my Kingsley Run marijuana patch, but tired feet and an empty canteen spoke more forcefully than nostalgia.

When I returned a few weeks later, I found where the old beech tree had stood, fallen, and returned to the soil to nourish the thicket of saplings that had grown from its seeds.

Christmas and the Constitution

At dinner one evening shortly after Thanksgiving, my stepdaughter spoke about the Christmas songs her first grade class was singing at school. I expected to hear about Christmas carols rooted in the simple joys of shared celebration. Despite its vulgar, rampant commercialization, Christmas remains a communal celebration of peace, joy, generosity, and kindness that transcends the strange, harshly judgmental worlds of both theology and superstition. It is a widespread cultural tradition, as well as a religious occasion. I would have had no problem with "Jingle Bells," or "Here Comes Santa Claus," or even "Silent Night."

[I observe Christmas even though I've been a Buddhist nearly all my adult life.]

But this first grade teacher was leading the class in songs that proclaimed Jesus (Jayzus!) to be the only alternative to hellfire and damnation. She was telling a roomful of six-year olds that all non-Christians would burn in hell for eternity (and that they deserve it) and requiring them to repeat her words with enthusiasm.

[My stepdaughter had already connected and, in some general sense, identified with Christianity partly as a simple matter of social ambience and partly through my devoutly Catholic father-in-law, who I'm confident didn't believe me to be evil and damned by virtue of my Buddhism.]

I requested a face-to-face meeting with the teacher and began the meeting by saying, "I have a problem with the Christmas songs you're requiring your class to sing."

"Do you have a particular religious objection to the songs?"

"No, it's not a religious issue."

The principal came in, introduced himself, and sat down.

I continued, "Would you agree that an important part of your mission here is to teach children to be respectful, law-abiding citizens?"

The teacher nodded, and the principal said, "Yes, of course."

"That's why I'm concerned about this teacher actively engaging her students in open displays of disrespect for the law of the land. This isn't about my religion, it's about the Constitution of the United States."

The now red-faced teacher began to say something, but the principal cut her off immediately as he turned to her and said, "If we fight him on this, we will lose."

I said, "Yes, you will, indeed."

The songs were eliminated from the curriculum.

Though I was glad to avoid a larger, more public conflict, the ease of my victory carried an uneasy implication: that the school's disrespect for both the Constitution and the right of parents to be responsible for the spiritual upbringing of their children had been conscious and deliberate, not merely naïve or thoughtless.

Old Trailers

Old trailers don't look merely weathered; they look battered. They have character, but it's not the kind of character that makes an old clapboard farmhouse reflect an old farmer's face weathered by sun, wind, laughter, and loss. Too often, an old trailer's character is that of a swollen-livered belly and a gap-toothed grimace. Or so it seemed to me in those days, and I had been inside enough of them to know.

This family had been receiving various combinations of welfare, Medicaid, and food stamps for a decade. I didn't like the guy, but that really didn't matter. I helped lots of people I didn't like and some that I loathed. Hell, I sometimes helped people I could have shot without a glimmer of conscience—that was my job; it's what a welfare caseworker did.

[I helped good people too. Most of the people I helped were good people, but they seldom left me with stories to tell. Their paperwork just flowed across my desk.]

I had already interviewed the "head of the household" and his wife, twice. The wife was barely coherent. Though I'm sure she had problems older than her marriage, I would have bet my paycheck that her husband beat her. I was a battered child and I knew too well the kind of twitches beatings wire into one's psyche, especially when bizarrely mixed with twisted love. I had seen her aura often, and many of those who wore it could see it in me. That's why they trusted me, and probably why her husband didn't like me any more than I liked him. He knew that I knew. But I had no evidence—nothing I could report or explain in a way that would mean diddley-shit to anyone with the authority to do anything about it. He knew that too. Frankly, the woman didn't matter much anyway. She was already a lost cause. But they had six children.

[It didn't take long, in my profession, to realize that you weren't helping louts, losers, bunglers, whack jobs, drunks, perverts, and the merely unlucky because they were unfortunate and/or deserving (though they were all unfortunate, and many were deserving). You were mostly trying to lighten the load on their kids, so their grandchildren might have a shot at being okay.]

They had to drive thirty miles one way to get to the welfare office for an eligibility review every three or six months, depending on what benefits they were receiving at any given time. The man worked off and on and reported changes faithfully. His jobs never lasted long. He always had the standard excuses—most of them were pretty good, and some of them were actually true, but he tended to get hired by assholes like himself who happened to be a little smarter and/or luckier. He was not unintelligent and presented himself as fundamentally competent.

I reviewed the case record and thought that someone ought to go out there and take a look. I also preferred that the family spend their money on more meaningful needs than gas to talk to me and sign new documents.

[There was also a State Game Land nearby where I could pull over, smoke a joint, and draw in my sketchbook for a while, afterward.]

The trailer was several miles back a rough dirt road in the northwest corner of the county and a stone's throw from the state line. When I pulled into the driveway, I knew I was stepping into something nasty before I opened the car door.

[I hated it when that happened.]

The half-decomposed dead chicken next to the front porch steps was an ugly omen, but I had seen worse.

The interior of the trailer looked like a concentration camp barracks. Most of the partitions had been torn out to make room for rough wooden bunks. The unfinished wood had been polished black by years of dirty hands. Every surface in the kitchen was encrusted with grease and the sink was heaped with moldy dishes.

The man was politely cooperative and well organized. Current utility bills, bank statements, employment office registration, etcetera were presented in perfect order. The only children present were the two oldest daughters, whose vibes completely creeped me out. I didn't ask why they weren't in school that day. (Plausible excuses for missing a day of school are easy to concoct.) I knew they were being molested, but just as the man's wife had no visible bruises, there was no objective evidence.

After the requisite signatures were obtained, I drove to the above-mentioned State Game Land, smoked the above-mentioned joint, and talked myself out of weeping and puking in the bushes. Back at the office, I stepped seamlessly into my competent, but cynical gonzo persona and authorized another six months of welfare, food stamps, and Medicaid.

[No matter what I thought of the asshole parents, the kids still needed to eat and go to the doctor when they were sick.]

That night, home alone in my studio trying to paint, I thought, "What the fuck, I could just drive out there in the morning, kick the door in, and shoot that less than worthless son-of-a-bitch." I really thought it—momentarily considered it as an option. I ruled it out because I didn't deserve where that would lead my life any more than those kids deserved to live in a private concentration camp in the boondocks of northwestern Pennsylvania.

I could stash my car in the State Game Land, hike across the intervening countryside with a rifle, hide 250 yards away in the tree line across the road, and center punch that piece of shit when he stepped out the front door. I might even get away with that one. A guy like that was bound to have enemies far more obvious than his caseworker. But yeah, that's crazy, and I talked myself down from it.

[Considering wild interventions and talking myself down from them was sometimes how I kept my heart from breaking. I also knew that the acute urgency of my emotions would subside by morning.]

I had learned to live with my scars well enough to be the caseworker and not the client, so I wept briefly, slept fitfully, and arose in the morning with a plan.

I called Warren County Children and Youth Services (WCCYS) and told them about the sheer, horrific squalor of the home. I didn't say anything about my other impressions and intuitions because I didn't want to diminish the facts I presented by appearing to overreact or pre-empt their professional judgment.

[My reputation in the world of local social services was far from pristine.]

WCCYS determined that the family needed counseling. Though it seems likely they understood there was a subtext to my referral, they needed harder evidence than my intuitive outrage.

A few weeks after the intervention that seemed pathetically mild to me at the time, the eldest daughter came forward to one of her teachers.

Did WCCYS's seemingly inadequate intervention give the eldest daughter the final bit of impetus she needed to come forward? I would like to think that— I'll take all the redemption I can glean from those fields of pathos, but that teacher surely deserves credit too.

The man was arrested. His wife went first to a mental institution and then to a group home. The children were placed in foster care. WCCYS would have endeavored to place the children with relatives, but I don't know what happened after I closed the case. I preferred not to know.

[Knowing was risky. Now and then, it might yield a brief warm and fuzzy moment, but if it didn't, it might piss corrosive darkness on my soul.]

Election Cycles

In the late nineties, I was president of the advisory board of the Jamestown Community Cultural Center, affiliated with Jamestown Community College (JCC), in southwestern New York. The centerpiece of the Community Cultural Center was Forum Gallery. Under the leadership of a bright, visionary, well-connected director, Forum Gallery brought to the college, community, and region an exhibition program far more bold and ambitious than anything commonly found outside of major urban centers.

When the Republican governor initiated his reflexive hatchet job on the state's higher education budget, the college administration informed the cultural center advisory board that the college was facing "tough choices." The administration regarded defunding the gallery as an easy, obvious, and relatively harmless place to begin working toward the needed austerity.

The board was disinclined to passive surrender. Our letters, e-mails, and phone calls resulted in several meetings with the college president and the chief financial officer, who were more interested in quelling controversy than in solving a problem they thought of as ours, not theirs. They tried to verbally lube the financial corncob, while gently urging us to bend over and shut up.

[Their technique works well with agitated dogs. They were really good at it.]

Most of my fellow board members were not well versed in the basic principles of political cynicism. Their various mixtures of angst and anger were readily calmed with slick smiles and soothing expressions of shared concern.

["I feel your pain."]

As we walked together to our cars after one such meeting, several board members spoke with naïve enthusiasm about how the chief financial officer truly seemed to understand where we were coming from. Bob stepped up his pace enough to take the lead and turned to face the group as we reached the edge of the parking lot. Everyone stopped.

[Bob was a faculty member of decades and chair of the English department. He was articulate, cultured, witty, and obese. Bob often spoke in parables that could seem bafflingly obscure to those who lacked the acuity to realize that's what he was doing.]

He said, "A dear friend of mine once bought an upright piano from the college. It was only a hundred-fifty dollars, and he was pleased and proud of his bargain. The piano sounded great, but a student had used a sharp instrument to scratch 'fuck you' in large letters across one end. He buffed the graffiti out and refinished the damaged area. It looked fine for a while, but two months later it said, 'fuck you' again. He repeated the buffing and refinishing and was once again proud of his bargain. A few weeks later, it said 'fuck you' again. He had the whole piano professionally refinished and was so pleased with the result that he opined that the piano was a great bargain even with the cost of refinishing. Six months later, it said 'fuck you' again."

Bob turned, walked a few steps to his car, and drove away.

Collective Gasp

In the wake of Donald Trump's surreal, minority victory, hordes of progressives and liberals are uttering countless variations on the theme, "I don't feel like this is my country anymore." And yes, I feel some of that too, even though I also realize that it's mostly an infantile conflation of raw emotion and reality.

[America is suffering from a collective overdose of simplistic thought.]

Other than a (hopefully) brief flourish of empowerment for bitter fools (giddily violent around its edges), nothing much has truly changed.

In my undergraduate days (late 1960s – early 1970s), the hippie culture in Clarion, Pennsylvania, where I was a student, was composed of many overlapping circles of friends that functioned in a zone somewhere between family and tribe.

[The social barrier between college and town was permeable at its interface with sex, drugs, and art.]

I became happily comfortable amidst a circle of bright, creative, gentle, generous people whom I regarded as a sort of extended family of choice. I felt at ease among them in ways I had never felt before.

[Personal qualities that made me a nerd in high school rendered me sexually attractive amidst the countercultural wildness rolling across the country in waves.]

This sense of empowered belonging played a large role in my ability to transit through some very dark times with my will to live, ability to love, and creative faculties intact.

[We were first-wave baby boomers and deep friendship offered warmth and security that had been (to varying degrees) missing from the homes presided over by our depression and war-damaged parents. We gave each other the reckless confidence that enabled our dissent.]

During that time and for a few years afterward, as we all wandered off into the post-college world of making a living and a life, I was entwined and entangled in a stormy, on-again-off-again relationship (fraught with mutual infidelities) with a woman who was also a member of my hippie clan.

After that stormy relationship finally completed its long unraveling, there were frequent moments of obvious social awkwardness in encounters with my old friends. I attributed this to various mixtures of circumstance and my perennial social ineptitude.

[Hey, it was inevitable that we would all grow apart. Right?]

When I married outside the tribe, my wife's beauty blinded most of my old friends to her intellect and her art. Though this caught me by surprise because I thought them more enlightened and less given to commonplace prejudices than that, I still trusted truth to become apparent to open eyes and minds. I tried to be patient because they were my people. Collectively, the facets of their personalities often reflected aspects of the kind of person I was, or at least tried to be.

[I built a new life in an old place—my hometown.]

I was a prolific letter writer and frankly, didn't give much thought to the lack of response my correspondence mostly received.

[I didn't keep score.]

Not everyone had a bureaucratic job that made letter writing an inconspicuous way to steal time from high-pressured work.

[I used stolen time to keep my inner wildness from drowning in structured responsibility.]

Gradually, as events and encounters unfolded, and I began to write consciously about my life, I realized that I had, in fact, never been a member of the clan of friends I had regarded as a truer family than blood. I had been kindly humored and tolerated as a true member's weird boyfriend. By the time this realization became clear, that part of my past was too far gone to merit the sharp pain of heartbreak it might have delivered many years earlier. But the dull ache of deep embarrassment became a part of the background noise of my story, and now, that folly, ache, and embarrassment is weirdly mirrored by my country.

[Nothing has changed, but so too has everything.]

The problem isn't so much what we have done as who we have been. It never was your country or mine.

[That was a poignant cocktail of naivety and vanity.]

It never will be your country or mine. But that doesn't mean you can't find your way home.

[Beware of darkness and greedy leaders.]

Give your allegiance to the confluence of your family (blood and/or spirit) and your watershed.

[Be kind to strangers.]

Legal Smile

After dinner at a downtown Durango brewpub, Dave and Caroline walked my wife, Terry, and me back to our motel. Our rambling conversation was energized by the intense affinity of new friendship. We paused in the back parking lot along the Animas River. Dave and I were talking about the sixties and (of course) the subject of marijuana and its personal impact came up. Dave and I both felt that marijuana had played a largely beneficial role in opening us to the truths of our lives. When the subject arose, I lowered my voice. Dave chuckled and said, "You don't have to do that—you're in Colorado." I hadn't realized I was lowering my voice—it was automatic. It was a deeply ingrained habit from more than forty years of post-hippie paranoia in the heavily policed East. The illumination of Dave's gentle prod rendered that reflex instantly emblematic of a whole broad range of small repressions by which my generation incrementally allowed itself to be silenced and shamed in relation to truly formative experiences. My first reaction was a laugh of pleasure at the banishment of fear —I was about to do something I had nearly lost hope in living to see: smoke marijuana legally.

In a sense, I have sometimes wished that I could classify marijuana as a very small thing, a pleasure like dark beer, cranberry scones, fresh garlic, or the smell of sage—wonderful things that could be given up without a truly meaningful impoverishment of life. The subliminal shame of legal fear renders trivialization attractive.

[Forbidden to articulate the meaning of certain experiences, we incrementally forget that they are indeed meaningful.]

Back in our motel room, when I lit a joint and passed it to Dave, my voice choked in a moment of complex emotion. This was not a trivial matter. It wasn't a cranberry scone. Marijuana was and is meaningful for me in ways that include, but also transcend, its well-known sensory delights. As a young man in the late sixties blundering naively out of an Appalachian backwater and a fiercely dysfunctional family into both college and a radically changing world, marijuana connected my thoughts to my senses in a new way that enabled me to see beyond the acculturated straitjacket of my background. It opened me to truth as a living presence in the world, not merely as the plethora of spoken and unspoken thou-shalt-nots of my upbringing or the complex, elegant intellectual constructions of my reading. I became an artist and as I struggled through the dark, aching swamp that is PTSD and chronic depression, being an artist saved my life.

[To keep opening wider and wider is my only faith. There are many ways to open, but sometimes grief and the scars of dead loves cripple one's options. It's a long story and another book.]

Please understand that in saying this, I'm not advocating for marijuana as a panacea for the world's ills, as old stoners sometimes do. People who get too far into any of several kinds of intoxication when too young tend to eventually find themselves thirty-four going on sixteen and clueless, and marijuana doesn't mix well with motor vehicles, chain saws, firearms, x-acto knives, power tools, and tall ladders. Shallow people tend to use it in shallow ways. Hot smoke in lungs already whacked by industry, tobacco, and minor nameless plagues is not an issue to be lightly dismissed. Where it's illegal, you must sometimes buy it from fools and you must fear the law.

Many of us accept that dark side as the unjust, yet worthy, price of breaking down artificial (though sometimes useful) barriers of definition between thought and perception, for the sweet vulnerability that allows the heart to both speak and listen through art, the profound truth(s) of loving sex, and to be able to see with (seemingly) perfect clarity the sheer, astounding, pervasive aliveness of the world. That's what I found in marijuana, and it rewired my head in permanent ways that nearly fifty years of well-educated skepticism have not undone.

That's why its illegality has been much more than merely a point of practical fear that has produced long periods of abstinence. Marijuana prohibition has been an official insult to the being I became in order to survive and then thrive beyond the legacy handed to me by a war-damaged father and a vicious, deranged mother. Nearly all my smiles, whether straight or stoned in the moment, are illegal in most states and frankly, it pisses me off. It has made me lower my voice countless times and in countless habitual ways that have tended to spill out of the baggie into the rest of my life.

But now, I'm too old for that shit. It's a hard habit to break, but I'm working on it.

A Change of Heart

The receptionist told me there was a man at the front desk who wished to apply for Medicaid. He said it was urgent and he wanted to speak with a supervisor before he even began the process. I recognized the name. Let's call him Mr. Doe.

[I had known him in grade school.]

Since I didn't think there was much chance that I was dealing with a crank, I broke with my usual policy of strictly following our organizational structure and the flow of our normal work process in the absence of a clear need for my direct involvement.

[In truth, most of my caseworkers were more competent than I was.]

When I saw the trapped-animal look in the man's eyes, I brought him to my office, rather than to an interview booth. He was quiet, dignified, and rational, but he was also a hair's breadth from panic.

Mr. Doe had inquired about Medicaid when he was first laid off from his job with little hope of getting called back, but was told that his income from unemployment compensation exceeded the maximum for his household size. His son had a congenital heart condition that was worsening steadily. Without a heart transplant the boy would die within a few months. Mr. Doe's health insurance had ended with his job, and now, even if he got called back or found a new job, his son's heart condition would be excluded from coverage as a "pre-existing condition." Since he had no means to pay for even a small portion of the enormous cost of a heart transplant, his son had been denied a place on the transplant list. Everything else about the boy's medical and social situation would place him very high on the transplant list, if ability to pay was no longer an issue.

I explained that if I classified his son as "presumptively disabled," a higher income limit would apply and that income eligibility for Medicaid was based on projected annual income. Since he had now exhausted a significant portion of his unemployment claim, his projected income would be based only on the remaining portion, which would make his family eligible, at least until he found a new job. I also explained that since past, unpaid medical bills could be used as a deduction from income in determining eligibility, a new job would, at worst, only interrupt his eligibility for the amount of time it took to incur medical bills greater than his excess income.

I also knew that the Pennsylvania Department of Public Welfare (DPW) wouldn't pay for a heart transplant. DPW was notoriously slow to enact changes in both coverage and fees and still classified increasingly commonplace heart transplants as an "experimental" surgery. Faced with having to look this man in the eye and hand his son a procedural death sentence, I decided to gamble and improvise. I helped Mr. Doe complete the written Medicaid application form, obtained all the appropriate signatures, and said, "Now, whom do I have to call to get your son on that transplant list?"

I've never seen such weight lifted from a person's countenance so instantly. I responded to his profuse expressions of gratitude as we walked backed to the reception area with, "This is what you've been paying taxes for all these years."

[I couldn't tell Mr. Doe my real intentions because, if I had, we would both have been guilty of conspiracy and fraud.]

After Mr. Doe left, I called the social service department at the hospital and told them that DPW would pay for the boy's heart transplant and that since his condition was perilous, it was vital that he be placed on the transplant list as soon as possible. The social worker on the other end of the line spoke with circumspect caution that revealed the skepticism I had expected so I said, "Look, I realize you have no way of knowing I am who I say I am. Let's hang up, and then you can go to your Commonwealth Directory and look up the number for DPW's Warren County office. Call that number and ask to speak to the person in charge of Medicaid eligibility. The operator will connect you to me, and we can take it from there."

[This was a classic con artist's gambit—divert the person's doubts away from the real issue of what DPW would cover to the easily resolved issue of my personal authenticity. If the whole thing went south, I could allow it to be

attributed to my incompetence. Since I didn't have a meaningful amount of ego invested in the job, taking that hit didn't matter much, as long as I didn't get fired.]

The social worker did as I suggested, and I assured him that I had just authorized full medical coverage, and that DPW would pay for the transplant.

The boy was placed on the transplant list and within a few weeks, he had a new heart.

The hospital got stiffed for a very large amount of money when they billed DPW, and the payment was rejected.

[It was vastly more than Mr. Doe could ever afford to pay. But his son was alive and couldn't be refused follow-up care.]

The strange mildness of the Executive Director's reprimand told me that he knew or strongly suspected what had actually gone down. I promised I would never do it again.

[I was lying.]

For several months afterward, I was tougher than I preferred to be. But no one starved as a result.

[Deliberate mistakes had to be carefully earned.]

Bartleby's Prayer

I stand to the left of the Democratic Party.

[Yes, to the left.]

My family of blood, choice, love, work, and marriage includes fellow Buddhists, Christians, Muslims, Hindus, Jews, atheists, agnostics, and thoughtless heathens.

[I am most comfortable among the first and last.]

Such diversity seems natural, but the Christians tend to squirm, pray aloud, and rant. The poignancy of their squirming renders it tolerable, but the rants stir an embarrassing meanness in my heart.

[I would prefer not to.]

My Father's Vest

Part One

I had been estranged from my parents for nearly seven years when they died two months apart in 2012.

My mother went first, and after her death released my father from her needs, his own downhill slide was rapid. His, at that point, undiagnosed lung cancer had spread to his bones—he had held on for her. But then, he still held on. He laid in his hospice room gasping for breath for two weeks after being told he had three to five days left. I went to the hospice house, took his almost limp hand in mine, and said, "What you and I believe about how the world works is very different, but I think one thing we share is that we'll probably meet again. I realize you tried to do the right thing and hope you realize that I did the same. When we meet again, let's try to take it a little easier on each other. That promise is the best we can do right now, so it's okay for you to let go."

He said something I couldn't decipher, but I pretended to understand, squeezed his hand, let go, and touched his shoulder. "Goodbye," I said, and left.

Three hours later, my son held his hand as he died.

I drank too much that evening, but I didn't mourn. I had mourned the loss of my father many years before they planted him. I went to his funeral, but I have never been to his grave.

Part Two

When my brother and I cleaned out my father's house, he had left behind a closetful of clothing well-suited for the outdoors in all seasons. I didn't want it. I didn't need to nurture memories entangled in complicated pain.

My father was a mean, generous, confused, brave, frightened asshole.

[He did heroic things in war and came home damaged in body and spirit.]

But I did claim a Woolrich vest—dark red and black plaid with fleece lining. It's a warm, comfortable, practical garment. I wear it often and like it for something mysteriously more than its merits. The vest has become part of small collection of special, comfortable clothing I wear when I want to hang out at home all day and immerse myself in writing. It feels lucky, like the stones I carry in my pocket, because the places they came from live so vividly in my heart—San Juan Mountains, Arches, Rio Grande Gorge, Vermont, Maine coast, Olympic Peninsula, Faroe Islands.

[Some people have photos in their wallets and/or on their phones—I have stones in my pocket. Places are to me, as more people probably ought to be.]

It's not merely a vest. It has something to do with my father that I don't understand yet. Perhaps both the poetry and psychology of my affection are as simple as the warmth that it gives, and he didn't. My father was a giver of heat, not warmth and certainly not light. The heat came mostly from a cold heart.

[Crippled by war.]

I am more like him than I want to be and I can't kill the kinship without jettisoning qualities I ought to keep.

[Keeping track of myself is a complex navigation.]

I have realized in retrospect that my father was, to some difficult to assess, but significant degree, intimidated by me after I became an adult. Though I am not sure when it began, some of our fierce confrontations in my thirties surely drove home the realization that he had passed his violence and darkness on to me, and that it had mutated in ways he didn't understand.

[He hid much of himself behind a peculiar mix of bluster and passivity.]

He sensed vague peril in realms where his rage once gave him power. In his later years, confusion and vague peril were probably leaking into his life through a multitude of cracks in the foundation. Life extracted a strange, sad bravery from him.

[My mother's dark craziness was a heavy cross to bear.]

Though forgiveness is complex and its many parts move and grow at different rates, I don't find it difficult.

[Moving forward unburdened is more challenging than it sounds.]

Affirmative Anger

En route to the photocopier, within potential earshot of the reception area and interview booths with open doors, I overheard one of the caseworkers I supervised, in conversation with a caseworker from another supervisory unit, refer to a client as a "goddamned queer."

[Despite strict confidentiality policies, when dealing with someone potentially violent or who didn't bathe, ever, leaving the interview booth door open could be a necessity.]

I didn't confront him immediately, because I wanted to consider my words carefully. I thought through my anger and formulated a practical, non-judgmental way to steer this caseworker in the right direction. As I approached his cubicle to ask him to come to my office, I heard the word "nigger" and thought, "Oh shit."

[My alter ego, Bartleby hated it when Reg got really pissed off.]

My nonjudgmental, practical, but firm methodology evaporated in the heat of my temper.

"Could you come back to my office, please?"

"Sure, what's up?"

"Close the door, please."

He closed the door and sat down.

[He knew something was up.]

"You're in this job, being paid with tax dollars, to help every eligible person who walks in the door. This morning, I heard you refer to one person as a 'queer' and another person as a 'nigger.' That is one hundred percent unacceptable."

"That was in private conversation."

"Well, I sure as hell didn't have any problem overhearing it. And I don't care what the context is, the next time I hear that kind of language from you, I'm gonna saddle you up and ride your ass right out of here. I'm serious, if we have to talk about this again, I recommend you have your union rep present."

A short while later, the Executive Director summoned me to his office. He wanted to know what made me think I could threaten to fire someone without bothering to consult him. He was right, and I apologized, even though my contrition was less than fully sincere. I had already witnessed an abundance of misogyny, which I was powerless to challenge, in his crude humor. I had, indeed, allowed my temper to override both protocol and procedure, but I had also been unsure that he would deal with the situation with the appropriate vigor.

[Though he was a flagrant womanizer, he wasn't a racist or a homophobe, but neither did he understand the complex power of ugly language.]

I was a forty-something father, who painted several hours every day and slept little. I found it frightening when the lines between noble moral outrage and the fierce temper bequeathed to me by a dysfunctional childhood became blurred.

[I needed my job.]

Love and Folly Along a Small Creek

Part One

Jack grew up in Pittsburgh. He played football in high school and on arriving at Clarion, a small state college in rural northwestern Pennsylvania, he joined a fraternity noted for its "Animal House" persona, but he was also gentle, bright, and an avid reader. When the countercultural wave of the late sixties swept into Clarion, he discovered art, cannabis, acid, Hinduism, and the forest in a tumultuous year that included the death of his father.

Jack and I shared an apartment through a semester of exuberant, youthful debauchery, wounded hearts (our own and others), and revelations.

After graduation, Jack took a state civil service test and was hired as a welfare caseworker in his native Pittsburgh. It was a convenient route to a new beginning, but the forest had gotten into his heart, head, and blood. The once comfortably familiar city had become abrasive and depressing (even though he would never stop loving it).

Meanwhile, I took the same test and paralleled Jack's path by getting hired as a caseworker in Warren, my hometown sixty miles north of Clarion, along the western edge of the Allegheny National Forest (ANF).

After a long absence, the dissonance of being a stranger in my hometown was much more burdensome than I expected or understood.

[My emotional life was entangled in lost love, social/political disillusionment, and bouts of deep sadness I hadn't yet identified as chronic depression. I found respite in solitude, but it was seldom joyful—I believed in it more than I loved it and only partially understood the importance of that distinction.]

On the weekends when I didn't go for an off-trail bushwhack wander in the ANF; I often drove back to Clarion to visit the remnants of my hippie semi-tribe who hadn't yet wandered off into the world of jobs and graduate school. I felt so alien in other parts of my life that, sometimes, old friends were the straw I breathed through to keep from drowning in youthfully romanticized existentialist despair.

[Long wanders in the forest reminded me that my roots went deeper than civilization.]

Jack began fleeing northward on every free weekend and diligently following the civil service postings for the counties in or adjoining the ANF as soon as he had permanent civil service status (not quite as solid as academic tenure, but nicely secure).

[Ease of transferring to another county was one of the major advantages of an otherwise stressful occupation. There's also a world of difference between being a welfare caseworker in Pittsburgh and being a welfare caseworker in a rural county like Warren.]

Jack and I went to The Summer Jam rock festival at Watkins Glen. The Band, The Grateful Dead, and The Allman Brothers played wonderfully, even incorporating the thunder into their jam when a storm broke out. But this was no Woodstock; something had changed. There was a strange, tense ambience that went far beyond the mud and rain. People weren't getting blissfully high; they were drinking too much tequila and puking in the mud holes.

[A skydiver attempted to parachute into the festival wearing flares for dramatic effect. The flares ignited his jumpsuit and burned him alive before he reached the ground.]

I forgot my corkscrew and had to pick a wine cork out with my hunting knife. We debated the nutritional value of cork while we passed the sun-heated bottle in the music-filled gaps between thunderstorms.

Jack took the first driving shift on the way home, while I quickly fell asleep in the passenger seat. I was wakened by Jack's frantic voice seeping through a fog of sleep, wine, and weed. "We have trouble. Get the dope, Reg; get the dope." An electric jolt of fear erupted from the realization that the pulsing red light was a police car, not a psychedelic dream. We had a bag of marijuana in the glove compartment, where Jack also had the vehicle registration.

As I opened the glove compartment and snatched our stash, I realized I had reacted so slowly we were already pulled over and the state trooper was looking straight at me in the beam of his flashlight. I quickly stuffed the baggie down into the crotch of my jeans.

"Where are you boys from?"

"Pennsylvania."

"I would like you to go back there as quickly as possible, but do not exceed the speed limit."

July 30, 1973: People went to Watkins Glen looking for Woodstock, wanting more to have been there than to be there.

I think what I witnessed was a turning point in the devolution of getting high into getting fucked up. Everyone who talks about the event has their own highly judgmental opinion, largely rooted in sources of dubious relevance. This bores the shit out of me.

Warren County was at the top of Jack's list. So when my (sort of) girlfriend (also a caseworker) moved on toward a new future, Jack applied for her vacant position and got the job.

While the ponderous gears of bureaucracy ground toward his transfer, Jack searched for an Allegheny forest homestead to buy (cheap). I assisted him, in a sense—genuinely by providing a place to stay on his house-hunting forays, and questionably with reactions no less uneducated than his own about prospective properties. I could go out in the woods and get meat, build a fire under the worst of conditions, navigate complex terrain without a compass, and roll joints while steering a car with my elbows. But in terms of practical skills for living within the conditions of civilization, I had only the same stoned instincts (lightly reinforced with bits of randomly acquired experience) that he had.

One evening, in a smoky Clarion apartment that had harbored a long succession of old friends and lovers, Bea, who had been my lover in a stormy relationship that ended the previous year, suggested a group expedition to the art museum in Cleveland. When I seconded the motion, I was implicitly volunteering to drive.

[I had a "good" job and a five hundred dollar, very used Oldsmobile Vista Cruiser station wagon with an interior slightly smaller than a dorm room.]

The consensus among the half-dozen passing joints around the table was, "Let's do it!"

Three weeks later, when I arrived at the appointed time with a full gas tank and a gram of opiated hash, the group had dwindled to only Bea.

[The museum's wonders delivered a much needed renewal of faith in the radiant energy of human creativity.]

I don't remember exactly how Bea and I ended up making out in a wooden waterfowl blind along Lake Erie. When I say it just seemed to happen like weather and flat tires, I don't mean that I couldn't have exercised more self-control; I mean that I didn't. I went with the flow, so to speak.

[We became a couple again more by default than by intention.]

I did, however, find this rekindled relationship far better than being alone and believed that it really could work out, though I didn't know what "working out" would mean or be.

October 21, 1973: We stand back to back and must each travel halfway around the world to meet. The first attempt had to span a few snowy blocks, the second a ten-mile hitchhike for me, and now it's sixty miles. If we can get far enough apart, we may fall in love. With each self-inflicted, painful farce our ardor increases.

Jack's quest was powered by a courageous mix of determination and naiveté. When he drove up one weekend to make an offer on a property, he hit a deer with his car on the way, the front porch had fallen off the house since his previous visit, and on his arrival, the owner's dog bit him, necessitating an emergency room visit and a tetanus shot.

[Good omens were scarce, indeed.]

The wild summer passed quickly as summers tend to do, and as autumn marched toward winter, Jack began to get desperate.

[Desperation is not a good state of mind for purchasing real estate.]

A realtor showed Jack a place that struck him with the full force of love at first sight. It was a camp far back on a single lane, unmaintained road along a beautiful little creek, Brown Run. That the camp hadn't been built for year-round habitation was a minor issue for us. We were returning to nature. Roughing it was no big deal. Our enlightened attitudes would enable us to prevail and prosper. Despite the sobering and cynical realities of a caseworker's profession, we were both still living in the confluence of our young male invincibility and hippie idealism.

October 29, 1973: I've observed Bea much, because she captures my attention so readily. She can only love a man when she has to steal his time from other commitments—job, art, or (unfortunately) another woman. She prefers the abrasions of conflict to the giddy risk of simply letting go and falling (or leaping) as I am all too prone to do. Though I know this will eventually split us apart, I blunder in deeper anyway.

I know no one who seems to see so beautifully.

November 6, 1973*: First snow.*

Daylong woods walk.

Silence and wind.

November 8, 1973*: They prefer fetishes to enigmas.*

When you momentarily allow empathy to proceed past it's normal checkpoints, you become like a medicine man handling a rattlesnake. The world is struck to its core with beauty and wildness.

November 13, 1973*: Visited Aaron yesterday—he and Lynette are getting married! Aaron was more gently human than I've seen him in far too long. Lynette fertilizes the finer edges of his humanity.*

And I was amazed at the work he had done: goat pens, greenhouse half built, chicken house, stone carvings—their new place is truly flowering.

Afterward I drove to Clarion, made love with Bea, and drove on late in the night without thoughts—only the fading echoes of the beauty I absorbed in the day: cold air, dreary March-like clouds, prancing wolfhounds, goats following Aaron to milking, old friends, longing gazes, and a welcome calm within me and Bea.

Jack was filled with longing for a new life close to the land a la Scott and Helen Nearing. I was just trying to get by. Though Jack's lovely ideas had great resonance with my own, I mainly just thought it would be better to live in a cabin in the woods than an apartment in town, and planting a garden in the spring seemed like a more sensible way to begin moving toward a more natural life than diving into a grand transformation.

[Sharing expenses with Jack sounded immeasurably better than paying a landlord.]

I was willing to put the photography that had come to seem like my heart's true vocation on hold for the possibility of a life that would feel more natural in ways I barely understood.

While Jack and I were making plans to move to the camp on Brown Run, Bea was wrapping up her degree in English. I thought and hoped our newly rekindled relationship might grow beyond its former limits. Being in love, while love was fresh and vibrant, simplified my life, rather than complicating it.

Our decision to live together hardly seemed like a decision at all. Carrying on our relationship across sixty miles of rural roads seemed absurd in the absence of compelling necessity.

Since there would be three people in the household and Bea had no income, I would be responsible for two thirds of the ongoing costs. Being the only wage earner in our life together wasn't something I regarded as generosity or a burden. It was just what needed to be done—the most direct solution to a relatively simple problem.

My "good job" was seriously crazy.

[A welfare caseworker labors on the stress-addled frontlines of social dysfunction.]

The Executive Director was a hard-drinking, womanizing manipulator of the type who gives Italian males a bad name. He was also kind, generous, and in need of male allies in a profession largely dominated by women. The insight that his own attitudes made the female majority in his staff a larger issue than it needed to be eluded him. I didn't care. I wanted adequate money, the woods, and a woman's love. Even my art was secondary to the simple comfort of love and nights beyond the abrasive sound of engines.

The time of banks, attorneys and paperwork that lay between Jack's decision to purchase the property and his legal possession of it coincided with the time of transition from late autumn into the cold heart of winter. No one had winterized the vacant cabin. We discovered the burst pipes and broken toilet when we began moving in. The propane space heater didn't work. The propane cook stove warmed the kitchen when we cooked, but couldn't be safely used for heating.

The old saying about cutting one's own firewood, that it "warms you twice" didn't quite apply here. The exertion of cutting and carrying was warming indeed, but burning the wood in the living room fireplace warmed only hands and feet held deliciously close to the flames. The fireplace created an up chimney convection that actually emptied heat from the cabin.

We were miles back in the woods, at the end of a one lane, unmaintained dirt road. Had our hardships been lesser, and the needs we struggled with less fundamental, Bea and I might have succumbed to petty frictions rapidly. Instead, our shared difficulties drew us together. Bea and I had the most harmonious time we would ever have living together. We were youthfully resilient and embraced our situation as an adventure.

[I didn't consciously abandon my journal, but for a couple of months there was no writing.]

Jack and I were small-town caseworkers living like Eskimos. We reeked of wood smoke, chain saw exhaust, and sweat. I had begun to seriously loathe my job, but I was also sufficiently addicted to its cash flow to endure my loathing and to cling, for a while, to Jack's dream of self-sufficient sustenance—we just had to make it to spring.

[Our colleagues were far more understanding than we recognized at the time.]

Jack radiated modest confidence and contagious enthusiasm when he spoke of his dreams, but he was quickly overwhelmed by unforeseen challenges and (relatively) small disasters. He could speak knowledgeably about wood stove efficiency and composting toilets, but couldn't make or implement a plan to fix the ice-cracked toilet and get heat in the cabin by whatever means were available here and now.

Beavers dammed the creek and flooded the road. It was six below zero inside the cabin one morning. Jack's car, parked a quarter mile away, was vandalized. A misstep with a chainsaw severed my bootlaces without cutting into boot or foot—I was unharmed, but breathless. Bea's cat licked her frozen water dish and leaped onto my chest looking frantic. Unrolling insulation in the attic, I stepped backward into the hatchway and fell into the living room. I walked into the kitchen during a brief thaw and noticed a sagging ceiling panel with a drop of water hanging on the peak of the sag. When I touched it with my finger, the entire panel disintegrated and flopped to the floor with a large accumulation of rodent debris from which exited a frightened mouse. Alcohol was frequent. Marijuana was constant.

We also had quiet nights resplendent with stars, long hikes with campfire lunches, and times when cutting wood was more deeply, fundamentally satisfying than any labor we had yet known.

[Electric space heaters devoured kilowatt dollars ravenously.]

As winter trudged onward, Jack began to withdraw. The deep silence of deep winter on Brown Run was sometimes transcendent for him but its cosmic indifference often ached, so he fled to havens of comforting distraction—mostly young women and coworkers who offered the use of their shower.

[I may have been entitled to be annoyed, but I wasn't. I felt passively unsurprised that things hadn't worked out as planned or intended.]

Bea spent most of her days alone at the cabin. My distaste for my job led me to put an idealistic gloss on her involuntary solitude. I assumed that those quiet winter days far back in the woods were simply wonderful for her, a great gift that, since I couldn't get it for myself, I was mightily pleased to give to her.

[This was stupidly naïve of me. While I'm sure she had some beautiful days out there, it seems equally likely that there was a large, lonely dark side to her isolation.]

By the time March arrived, Bea and I knew we had to get out. Jack's talk about his intended life transformation began to sound increasingly hollow. For me, living on Brown Run had become an expensive enterprise that was consuming all my income and devouring my modest savings. We had to get out while I still had enough money left to get us out.

March 1, 1974: Jack remains incommunicado, but not merely that—waves of discomfort pour visibly through him. He disappears mysteriously as often as he can. I think I'll have to jump off this situation as from a sinking ship. Jack's strange mixture of restlessness and passivity is not what he needs to make this thing work. (Meanwhile living here has eaten every cent I've made and then some.) Watching his dream implode, he is blind to everything but his own suffering and confusion. He waits to be inspired, not realizing that one acts in order to become inspired, not because one is already inspired.

When Jack returns from Pittsburgh this weekend, I have to at least make my intentions clear. I hope I can afford to pay him enough to make him feel fairly treated in light of my backing out. I would rather take an unfair loss than leave him feeling cheated, but I also have to go on from here and I need to make photographs again.

Jack and I each presented our written personal accounting of our contributions to the communal living situation—something we should have been doing regularly from the beginning. Everything had been so haphazard and offhand that our accountings couldn't possibly match, but mutual trust, and apathy in the realm of keeping score resuscitated a friendship that might have died out, had I remained at Brown Run.

In the seemingly luxurious ease of an apartment, the first serious tensions arose in my relationship with Bea. That she needed more people, and needed them more than I, became one of the chronic conflicts we would never successfully resolve.

April 16, 1974: How much time can you kill before you are overwhelmed with the stench of rotting, dead hours?

May 3, 1974: Bea released a flood of reasonless tears last night. I tried to comfort her, but did a poor job of it.

Intermission

I didn't return to Brown Run for six years. I feared its wild beauty would be overwhelmed by memories of ill-defined failure and disillusionment. I had gotten to know that valley as a friend and sometimes I missed it, but there were other places to hike and roam with much less baggage.

I wandered off to Chicago for a year, gave up photography, fell wholly in love with painting, returned to working as a caseworker in Warren, Pennsylvania, transferred to another county, became a freelance buyer and seller of precious metals, and proposed to the love of my life, who also happened to be married to a good friend. She said, "Yes."

Part Two

Terry exited her first marriage as spring began to blossom into summer. More than three years of heavily constrained desire and the sheer magnitude of our mutual passion made us enormously hungry for each other—for each other's bodies certainly, but also for the intimate, intricate details of life and memory.

[There is an abundance of generically sound advice against making major life changes under the influence of sexual enthrallment. We took a large, wild gamble when we leaped so deeply into devotion so quickly.]

Sharing places of past love and transformation constituted a marriage of sorts. We announced our love to the world itself and declared previous connections null and void by replacing the associations of old memories with new ones fervently imprinted with our love. Our lives converged now in a vast terrain of formerly unshared living, with the floodgates of desire suddenly wide open.

Despite its history of hardship and folly, Brown Run remained a place remembered for its transformative epiphanies of natural beauty. Though my life there six years earlier had rapidly devolved into a muddle of clueless idealism, romantic distraction, and way too much marijuana, my day-to-day life then had been a more constant immersion in the large and small beauties of a particular place than any I had known before. The dysfunctions of the time faded, but the resonance of that little valley's wildness remained vividly alive in my heart.

So, on a bright summer day, I took Terry to Brown Run.

We hiked up the valley bottom by following the creek's edge through the cool shade of hemlocks and wading in the creek when it transited small meadows filled with chest-high weeds. We walked at a leisurely pace, and spoke of my Brown Run memories and our present wonders, until a certain small meadow announced itself by inscrutable means, as the place to cease from the mandatory attentions of walking and pour our attention into each other. We shed our clothes and frolicked in a creek so cold and sun so brightly hot that, rising from the water, we felt its sudden evaporation like a cooling breeze.

June 22, 1980: A walk along Brown Run with Terry—wild strawberries and infinite sky—cold water—kisses—sunlight on tanned bodies and golden hair—wandering talk and loving presence—we paused in a sunlit place along the stream to smoke and sit—immersed ourselves in achingly cold water tingling every cell to bright life and made love with and in the utter intensity of this wild summer.

Our love and hunger reached an unexpected critical mass that day. Afterward, we made love in the forest, standing in creeks, in moving cars, in the warmth of campfires, in moonlight, bright sun, and shade. We were passionately oblivious and sometimes inadequately surreptitious as we reclaimed old territories of both passion and place with reckless abandon. We probably left a trail of embarrassed friends and family in our wake.

[Volition was only marginally involved. The very act of stepping (again and again) into that current of surrender was bliss more ecstatic than orgasm.]

When we walked back downstream to my truck, Brown Run was truly a new place. It belonged to my life with Terry now. Its wildness seemed freshened and fertile.

July 9, 1980: I rose early to weed my embarrassingly jungle-like garden and mow the lawn in growing sun—took pleasure in simple physicality and sweat—showered, ate, and retreated to my studio. I smoked and wrestled down my self-doubt and stepped out onto that old tightrope again to paint in the radiant colors of Terry's kiss in summer sun.

Justice and Savagery

That governments should not be in the business of putting people to death via an organized, judicial process seems so self-evident that I'm hardly interested in debating it as an issue. But since it is apparently not thus self-evident to many people who otherwise appear to be civilized, perhaps I should explain my viewpoint.

It's not necessary to offer up pages (and perhaps graphs) of well-documented statistics, case studies, and anecdotal evidence to support my contention that human beings and their various programs of social organization are fallible.

[It's damned near a priori.]

In a system of law that allows capital punishment, the execution of innocents is not a question of "if" but of how many and how often. If you insist that this is simply a necessary matter of quality control, then we have to discuss the error rate for the very simple reason that human perfection is unattainable. What's the acceptable percentage of innocents among those executed by due process of law? One percent? Ten? Fifteen?

[Zero seems both obvious and naive.]

And then, of course, there's the matter of deciding which crimes deserve the ultimate penalty? If we grant that the perpetrators of certain crimes are, indeed, thus deserving, however short the list of crimes may be, we merely circle back around to quality control. But frankly, if you believe you have the requisite wisdom to decide whether another human being has a right to be alive, that they are so far beyond the possibility of even partial redemption that they should be put down like a rabid dog, are you not engaging in exactly the kind of psychopathic arrogance that theoretically characterizes those who should be thus put down?

[Brutality damages the humanity of the perpetrator. The brutality of a democratically elected government degrades the collective humanity of the nation.]

My argument here has nothing to do with sympathy for serial killers, child molesters, or Dick Cheney. Though there are people in the world, whose guilt is truly beyond all possibility of doubt, whom I could, without troubling my conscience, put on their knees and blow their brains out, this is a personal flaw, not a political principle. The reason it is a personal flaw is not the harm that would be done to someone who lives deep in the spectrum of genuine evil. It is a personal flaw because it arrogantly presumes that my negative emotions have philosophical stature on a par with moral principles.

[Christian culture's grounding of morality in punishment is an even larger spiritual failure than the absurd metaphysical swill it spews in torrents. If you want to search out the source(s) of our crazy excess of social violence, start there, with an inquiry into the value, efficacy, and consequences of punishment.

Is good behavior primarily a product of fear?]

Cruelty and death cannot be redeemed or compensated by cruelty and death.

[Justice is a compass bearing by which our collective will can steer toward peace. It is not a place or a thing.]

Only the gift of good work can counterbalance transgression.

Tiona, Pennsylvania, 1977

On a summer morning, I drove to my friend Hartwell's forest-edge home for a solitary hike. Hartwell was moving a slab of rock the length and width of a large refrigerator and half the thickness by using an iron pry bar to roll it a few inches at a time on small pieces of log. When I asked if he needed help he said, "No, there's not much you could do—the damned thing is too big for us to pick up." When I returned shortly before sunset, he had moved the rock perhaps thirty feet and was still working.

A week later, the rock was nowhere to be seen. I never learned why he needed to move it.

The Silence of the Memes

Google dictionary:
meme
/mēm/
noun
noun: **meme**; plural noun: **memes**
an element of a culture or system of behavior that may be considered to be passed from one individual to another by nongenetic means, especially imitation.

> a humorous image, video, piece of text, etc., that is copied (often with slight variations) and spread rapidly by Internet users.

I was working on a writing project that had been written in fragments that I was now trying to stitch together into something whole. Mentally arranging and rearranging the multiple pieces was tiring work, and when I needed a break; a couple of clicks took me to the effortless distraction of Facebook.

Casually scrolling through my news feed, I saw a meme posted by a real world friend. It gave me a little momentary surge of righteous anger because I shared my friend's outrage and disgust with both the president and the particular abuse of power referred to in the meme. I clicked "like" and scrolled on.

A few minutes later, I went to the basement to move a load of clothes from the washer to the dryer and as I descended the stairs, a thought arose, "Wait a minute, that wasn't true."

When I returned to my desk, I posted the following on Facebook, in response to the dishonest meme:

I am appalled seeing fellow well-left-of-center folks getting so worked up about President Dumpsterfire that they spew forth memes and rants that play as loose with truth and history as the liar-in-chief and his cognitively challenged minions—even folks who REALLY ought to know better. Even if Jabba the President gets dragged away kicking and screaming in cuffs and leg irons, it'll be a Pyrrhic victory at best if the sanctity of truth is trashed in the process. The scariest thing about any enemy is that they can make you become like them (that's the real reason for turning the other cheek—to refuse to become a mirror image of one's enemy). Climate change and the dysfunctional patriarchy that caused it are about to eat us for lunch, folks--we have to get this right or we may have to rebuild a civilization before we get another chance. It really is that serious—this is no time to fuck around.

There's much more to this than the integrity of our side or any side. The power of truth as a political force is at stake. Until very recently, I have been able to view outrageous displays of inhumane, misguided, and/or corrupt socio-political dysfunction with a measure of patience and resignation, because I have always (even in the depths of Vietnam-era protests) believed that the truth will prevail, that it rises by natural law as inexorable as gravity.

[Natural law operates without regard for human needs, desires, or expectations.]

My belief in truth has been an essential part of the foundation of my ability to love my fellow human beings in a broader sense than my affection for a few individuals.

[What would it mean to surrender that faith in my eighth decade on Earth?]

The text of that meme contained a false statement presented as historical fact. The man who posted it is a very good human being, who is a genuine blessing to his community and impeccably honest in other aspects of his life. The bothersome aspect of this, beyond the simple embarrassment of having carelessly endorsed a falsehood, is that a surge of righteous outrage elicited with a skilled, but heavy hand leaves a stronger psychological imprint than the calm, rational recognition of falsity later on. A lie that affects a person in its intended way regardless of whether they do or do not recognize its falsity gets right to the heart of everything I call "insidious." We are being bombarded by these things. We are being shaped by them.

We, the people, are being collectively duped into full participation in the systematic degradation of the meaning and value of truth itself.

[We have met the Donald and he is us.]

How many such falsities have I carelessly endorsed over the years, without ever having that little epiphany later on? Yes, I could remedy that by paying more attention and fact checking before responding, but social media already seize more of my time and energy than I can justify with any kind of cost-benefit analysis, and I can't think of a much more complete waste of life than time spent fact checking memes. They simply aren't worthy of that kind of attention—the medium is inherently simplistic, even if it is occasionally elevated to simplicity by small eruptions of genius or redeemed with laughter.

[The redemption of laughter wears very thin when it enables more self-righteousness than courage.]

To partake of the realm of memes one must swim in an undifferentiated torrent of bullshit, chickenshit, horseshit, and batshit from which one must seek and retrieve thinly scattered gems. I don't have time for that shit.

[The intuitive metaphors are all excretory.]

The very idea of truth is melting away in a torrent of carelessness and falsity. The pathos is heavy. It damages us and it is unbearably sad that we consume it with such gusto when our refusal to partake would end it.

[Simplistic thinking is a common craving among the desperate and the lowest common denominator is a powerful force in the world of social media.]

I'm not sure how to seek shelter from the shit blizzard without completely disengaging from social media, which I'm not (yet) prepared to do. I have made human connections online that I value highly, but I loathe the way things that are less than meaningless to me seize a meaningful portion of my mental bandwidth without my consent—the intellectual equivalent of being groped.

[It's creepy and we feel kind of queasy and uneasy, but the voice is soothing and it brings us kittens and candy.]

I don't have a solution; I'm still struggling to find a balance that I'm unsure is possible. But simplistic expressions supported by dubious assertions of factuality have claimed a portion of my life, and the loss feels like theft. It's difficult not to resent being ripped off, but of course, my resentment is as pointless as the lies being spread by honest people with good intentions.

[The disconnect between personal and social morality is one of several holes through which evil leaks into the world.]

I could close my social media accounts and go online only to purchase what I can't buy locally, submitting my writing, and checking the weather report. It's tempting, but the problem is that the suppurating pustule on the ass of humanity that is political power in the USA is no longer a distant abstraction, and while I'm old enough to be spared the worst by mortality, many of those I love are not.

I carry a deep debt of blood, grief, and hope to sustain at least my ability to speak truthfully, even if my use of it is beset with blunders.

Memes (etcetera) are not communication, they are thefts of attention. Their only real content is the reflexive triggering of simplistic emotional responses. Fear and outrage are easily tweaked.

[They are synthetic howls.]

Despite clever postures of righteousness, the meme says nothing at best and often horribly less than nothing. The essence of vacuity, it is silent in a terrible, cynical way.

I'm not comfortable being the kind of person who dismisses a whole medium or genre across the board, but that's what I'm going to do—stop responding. Ceasing to respond is not easy with something ubiquitous; a tangled web of habits will have to be carefully unraveled. But I'm going to do it—train myself to breeze right by that shit without responding. That's not merely a quirk of personal preference; it's a civic duty.

For me, it's the only alternative to going dark.

I have begun writing letters to geographically distant friends.

[With a pencil.]

The Stones I Carry

The stones in my pocket help keep me honest by being stronger and truer than my words. They tether me to places that seem radiant with spirit and resonant with truths that cannot be uttered.

[I don't know what "spirit" fully means, but in the absence of a better word, I accept its ambiguity. The difference between a mossy, water-smoothed and shaped marble boulder in southwestern Vermont and a paved parking lot anywhere transcends both semantics and philosophy. That difference is what I call spirit, and it keeps me alive.

Spirit's manifestations are many, and I can't perceive them all, which is why I decline the violent exclusivity of belief. Instead, I try to live in the confluence of my heart's strange mysteries and the land's implacable wildness.]

In a sense, I carry those places in my pocket, and that helps me to carry them in my heart.

Weminuche Wilderness Area

Schoodic Peninsula

Rio Grande Gorge

Arches National Park

Taconic Range

Olympic Peninsula

Saksun

[Colorado, Maine, New Mexico, Utah, Vermont, Washington, Faroe Islands.]

One morning in the mid-1990s, when I was getting ready for a busy office day and had to teach in the evening, I was suffering from a lingering cold and felt harried and overwhelmed. My weary distress was pretty obvious. As I was leaving, my son, Oren (eleven years old then), gave me a white pebble. "Here, carry this with you. It's from Gifford Woods," he said. And through that weary stressful day and many days to come, it was a comforting presence.

[Gifford Woods State Park, near Killington, Vermont, was a favorite camping place on the summer wanders that gave me lifesaving respite from a stressful career, and rendered Oren's vision of the world both broader and more intimate.]

I carried the stone Oren gave me in my pocket for a dozen years. Its sharp edges were worn smooth by coins, keys, pens, and the smooth, rounded quartz pebble from my ancestral territory that soon joined it in my pocket.

[The Tionesta watershed of the Allegheny Plateau.]

Once, I left Oren's stone in a special place in the woods (where the resident ravens knew me and I became acquainted with a large, ghost-like coyote whom I regarded as brethren) for most of a summer.

[Nowadays one must hike through an oil field to get there.]

When I retrieved it, I imagined it to be somehow infused with the spirit of that place mingled with the spirit of the Green Mountains.

[It became poetry made of stone.]

When Oren was fifteen, a floatplane carried us far out into the tundra of northern Quebec where we hunted caribou with longbows and homemade arrows.

Sitting near a well-used caribou trail on a large island in the Pons River, I felt an unexpected wave of deep, childlike homesickness.

[We were so incredibly far from everything known and dearly loved in a staggeringly beautiful, but also incredibly harsh, land.]

Holding the quartz pebble from the beloved landscape of my ancestry and birth transformed poignancy into comfort and fond nostalgia. The pastoral gentleness of my native Alleghenies seemed alive in that smooth, round piece of white quartz.

After I killed a caribou on the island a few days later, I left the pebble there. It seemed intuitively necessary.

[We brought home our winter's meat and through it, took the tundra into our blood, muscles, and bones.]

The pebble I left on the island was soon replaced by another that was, in turn, left in a faraway place. I began gathering pebbles on my wandering hikes (often retracing routes gleaned from my great-grandfather's journals) for the purpose of leaving them on my travels beyond my homeland.

There are quartz pebbles from the Tionesta watershed in Arkansas, Colorado, Delaware, Faroe Islands, Florida, District of Columbia, Georgia, Illinois, Indiana, Iowa, Kansas, Kentucky, Maine, Maryland, Massachusetts, Michigan, Minnesota, Missouri, Montana, Nebraska, New Brunswick, New Hampshire, New Mexico, New York, North Carolina, Oklahoma, Ontario, Quebec, South Carolina, Tennessee, Texas, Utah, Vermont, Virginia, Washington, and West Virginia. There are stones from all those places scattered about in the Tionesta watershed of the Allegheny Plateau.

[I cherish the invisible histories of my stones—the imagined millennia of unknown events they had "witnessed."]

Sometimes, I carried a stone in my pocket for a year or two and then returned it to where it had been found.

[I didn't have a particular idea of what this meant or should mean.]

When my son went away to college, I left quartz pebbles from home outside every place he lived during those four years. It was a kind of prayer for his protection—not to a God whose existence I doubt, but to the Earth.

[The Buddha called the Earth to witness.]

When I was younger, I thought ritual or ceremony engaged without clear knowledge of its meaning was self-evidently absurd, maybe even stupid. But now, as I wander into my eighth decade, meaning often seems illusory and drug-like, while honoring affection seems like a better route toward truth.

[I left the last quartz pebble from my pocket at the summit of Dorset Peak, in southwestern Vermont, after I realized that despite the beloved happenstance of birth and ancestry, the oil, gas, and timber ravaged Alleghenies were no longer my home and would never be again.]

In the leather shoulder bag I made to carry my notebooks, I keep a palm-sized deerskin pouch. Twenty years ago, when it was new, it was a rich golden ochre color. Now, after being carried on my travels, held in my palm in times of danger and stress, and anointed with dirt, sweat, and Montana Pitch Blend, it's earthier looking.

[Though I certainly knew what a medicine pouch was in indigenous American culture, I didn't think about that with regard to my pouch. It began as a simple way to carry a few special objects with me when I traveled or wandered in the woods. Then one day, a friend saw me tuck it into a pocket on my daypack and asked, "Is that your medicine pouch?" I hesitated a second and said, "Yeah, I guess so."

I feel a little uncomfortable calling it that because the weird pretensions of white wannabe Indians activate my gag reflex, but the association couldn't be erased once it was made, and thinking of the pouch in that way brought clarity, not fog.]

I've shown the contents of the pouch to fewer than a half-dozen people. Once in a conversation with a cousin, I used it to explain what suffices for religion in my life and mind. I said, "I carry my church in my bag. Here it is." I untied the drawstring and took out the contents one piece at a time.

First, another much smaller deerskin pouch containing a small bronze Buddha sitting in the "Calling the Earth to Witness" pose. This pouch is made from the hide of a deer I hunted, killed, and ate. It is lined with soft fur from Buddy, a lilac Siamese cat who was one of the best and truest friends of my life.

A second tiny pouch contains an Archaic period arrowhead found by my nephew in what was once Seneca Indian territory. He gave it to me in appreciation for the Osage longbow I made for him.

A sharp-cornered, roughly pyramidal stone from the tundra of northern Quebec.

A pale brown, speckled pebble from the Taos Pueblo. An artisan there who made a crucifix we bought as a gift for my devoutly Catholic and very ill father-in-law advised me to choose a pebble from the (then) dry creek bed and carry it as a prayer.

The white pebble from Gifford Woods that my son gave me many years ago.

Two smooth quartz pebbles from the Tionesta watershed—one ovoid and one heart-shaped.

A small, white stone from the Faroe Islands, a place that sings to my spirit and holds my heart as no other.

A smooth, gray stone with white veins that I found at Little Hunter Cove on Mount Desert Island, where a sunny oceanside epiphany inspired me to moderate the chronic workaholism that was killing me.

A smooth, black stone, the origin of which I've forgotten.

[I can feel the ocean in it.]

A rough piece of white marble from the Taconic Range in southwestern Vermont.

A small copper heart.

[A gift from my wife.]

My father's World War II dog tags. They accompanied him through a time of great horror and peril that left him deeply damaged, and they remind me of the long, strange journey of forgiveness I must travel as his son.

[Both my father and his generation require a great deal of forgiveness. I hope I will not need quite so much.]

Two years after my adventure with Oren, I returned to the far north with a friend. Glassing from a hilltop on our second full day of hunting, we saw a waterfall on a stream connecting two lakes a hundred yards apart. We had to take a closer look. It was one of those special places that command an involuntary hush, where you can feel the very heartbeat of a whole region. Whether together or separately, we took a few minutes each day to just be there. We heard wolves howling every morning and every day we saw fresh wolf tracks above the waterfall.

Several years before, while helping rescue artifacts from a flooded basement in a building owned by the Warren County Historical Society, I picked up a Seneca Indian turtle shell rattle, and three small pebbles fell out. I couldn't find a way to put them back in. Exactly how they had fallen out was a small, but genuine, mystery. I put them in my medicine pouch.

I tossed the three pebbles, along with a quartz pebble from the Allegheny Plateau, into the pool at the bottom of the waterfall. Unexpected shivers rippled up my spine. Boundless awe and love of the tundra, mixed with a heavy feeling of being terribly alone and immensely far from home, welled up inside of me.

When writing alone in my journal or notebook, especially when camping, traveling, or in the little cabin in the woods near our house, I usually lay out some of the contents of the pouch before me—often just the bronze Buddha and perhaps one or two stones. It helps my writing by ritually separating my thoughts from the plethora of distractions that is my daily life and grounding me in the possibility of truth, in much the same way that the Buddha was thus grounded by touching the Earth.

[Mystical explanations are so vulnerable to doubt that they tend to degrade mystery into confusion.]

I clutched the pouch in my coat pocket when the airplane I was riding in missed the runway and nearly hit a mountain, again a few days later, in a floatplane landing on a choppy wilderness lake, and in many other times of danger and/or distress. I have no particularly insightful explanation for the comfort it provides me.

I accept the gift of its comfort in much the same way that I accept the gifts of venison, blue skies, campfires, and my wife's love.

All those gifts and many more are spiritually evocative to me, but I crave and cherish the evocation far more than the gift.

I love its dancing lightness and don't want to weigh it down with a footnote explanation or imaginary claim of possession to be dragged along like a ball and chain.

[A few pebbles in my pocket suffice as a gentle tether to the Earth.]

Acknowledgments

I am grateful to the following journals in which a number of these essays were published for the first time:

Awakened Voices Magazine, Bird's Thumb Journal, The Chaos Journal of Personal Narrative, Cicatrix: A Journal of Experimentation, Dark Matter Journal, Heartwood Literary Magazine, The Remembered Arts Journal, River Teeth, Rivet Journal, Route 7 Review, Sky Island Journal, Star 82 Review, Tiferet Journal, Timberline Review, Traditional Bowhunter Magazine, Wanderlust Journal, Whitefish Review.

About the Author

Reg Darling lives in Bennington, Vermont. His spiritual advisor is a cat.